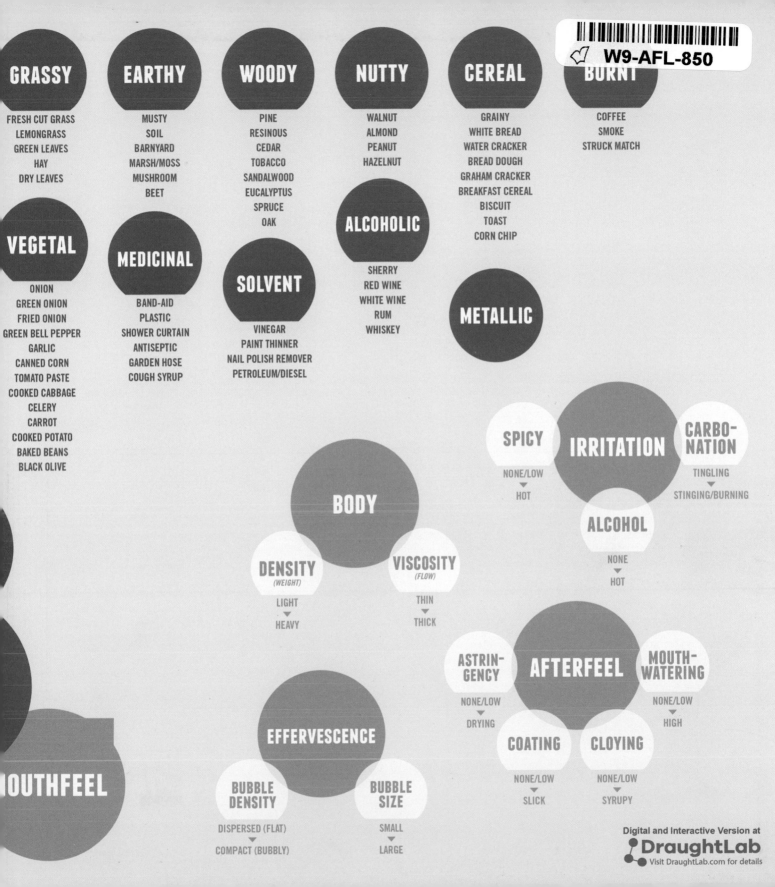

GRASSY
- FRESH CUT GRASS
- LEMONGRASS
- GREEN LEAVES
- HAY
- DRY LEAVES

EARTHY
- MUSTY
- SOIL
- BARNYARD
- MARSH/MOSS
- MUSHROOM
- BEET

WOODY
- PINE
- RESINOUS
- CEDAR
- TOBACCO
- SANDALWOOD
- EUCALYPTUS
- SPRUCE
- OAK

NUTTY
- WALNUT
- ALMOND
- PEANUT
- HAZELNUT

CEREAL
- GRAINY
- WHITE BREAD
- WATER CRACKER
- BREAD DOUGH
- GRAHAM CRACKER
- BREAKFAST CEREAL
- BISCUIT
- TOAST
- CORN CHIP

BURNT
- COFFEE
- SMOKE
- STRUCK MATCH

W9-AFL-850

VEGETAL
- ONION
- GREEN ONION
- FRIED ONION
- GREEN BELL PEPPER
- GARLIC
- CANNED CORN
- TOMATO PASTE
- COOKED CABBAGE
- CELERY
- CARROT
- COOKED POTATO
- BAKED BEANS
- BLACK OLIVE

MEDICINAL
- BAND-AID
- PLASTIC
- SHOWER CURTAIN
- ANTISEPTIC
- GARDEN HOSE
- COUGH SYRUP

SOLVENT
- VINEGAR
- PAINT THINNER
- NAIL POLISH REMOVER
- PETROLEUM/DIESEL

ALCOHOLIC
- SHERRY
- RED WINE
- WHITE WINE
- RUM
- WHISKEY

METALLIC

BODY

DENSITY *(WEIGHT)*
LIGHT ▼ HEAVY

VISCOSITY *(FLOW)*
THIN ▼ THICK

SPICY
NONE/LOW ▼ HOT

IRRITATION

CARBO-NATION
TINGLING ▼ STINGING/BURNING

ALCOHOL
NONE ▼ HOT

MOUTHFEEL

EFFERVESCENCE

BUBBLE DENSITY
DISPERSED (FLAT) ▼ COMPACT (BUBBLY)

BUBBLE SIZE
SMALL ▼ LARGE

ASTRIN-GENCY
NONE/LOW ▼ DRYING

AFTERFEEL

MOUTH-WATERING
NONE/LOW ▼ HIGH

COATING
NONE/LOW ▼ SLICK

CLOYING
NONE/LOW ▼ SYRUPY

Digital and Interactive Version at
DraughtLab
Visit DraughtLab.com for details

DRINK BETTER BEER

DRINK BETTER BEER

DISCOVER THE SECRETS *of the* BREWING EXPERTS

★

Joshua M. Bernstein

STERLING EPICURE

New York

STERLING EPICURE
New York

An Imprint of Sterling Publishing Co., Inc.
1166 Avenue of the Americas
New York, NY 10036

ISBN 978-1-4549-3311-3

Distributed in Canada by Sterling Publishing Co., Inc.
c/o Canadian Manda Group, 664 Annette Street
Toronto, Ontario M6S 2C8, Canada
Distributed in the United Kingdom by GMC Distribution Services
Castle Place, 166 High Street, Lewes, East Sussex BN7 1XU, England
Distributed in Australia by NewSouth Books
University of New South Wales, Sydney, NSW 2052, Australia

For information about custom editions, special sales, and premium and corporate purchases, please
contact Sterling Special Sales at 800-805-5489 or specialsales@sterlingpublishing.com.

Manufactured in China

2 4 6 8 10 9 7 5 3 1

sterlingpublishing.com

Interior design by Gavin Motnyk

A complete list of image credits appears on page 210.

Parts of "Nice Package" were adapted from "So Metal," published by *Imbibe* magazine.

Parts of "The Great American Zero" appeared in different form,
"Seeing the Light," also published by *Imbibe* magazine.

"Wholesale Change" was adapted from "Wholesale Change,"
published by *BeerAdvocate* magazine.

Parts of "Consistency Is Not a Four-Letter Word" were adapted from
"The Imitation Game," also published by *BeerAdvocate* magazine.

The profile of Jensen Cummings appeared in different form, "Brewed Food Rewrites the Rules of
Culinary Fermentation and Beer Dinners," published by *Draft* magazine.

"One Is the Magic Number" appeared in different form, "The Power of One,"
also published by *Draft* magazine.

To everyone in the beer industry

forever proving that a single beverage

contains endless complexities

★

CONTENTS

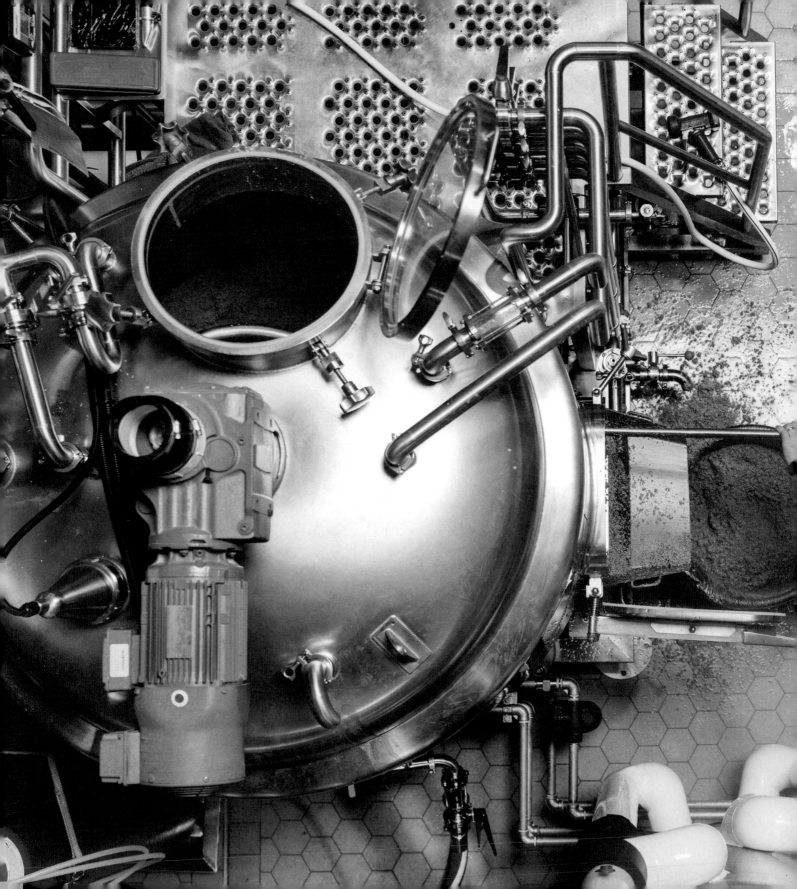

PREFACE

There was no mistaking me for a drinking-age adult. I was twenty and favored chunky plastic black glasses—I was channeling Elvis Costello—my hair as tall and spiky as wetland reeds. I also had a pierced tongue. It was a misguided style move that mainly led to chipped teeth, through which I lied at the drive-through booze barn.

Countless like it dotted my hometown of Dayton, Ohio. You drove in and ordered sugary sodas, candy, cigarettes, crunchy snacks, wine, and beer; every vice available from the comfort of your car. This particular drive-through was different due to a lax attitude toward checking IDs. This was the late '90s, and transgressions more easily flew beneath the legal radar. There were no cameras tracking every move, no social media revealing all.

I pulled my hand-me-down Nissan Stanza, a tan and boxy minivan with sliding doors, into the drive-through with a mission to buy a dozen 40-ouncers of King Cobra malt liquor. My friends and I were on spring break from college and headed on a road trip to Texas, Colorado, and New Mexico, lands where surely no liquor existed.

"A case of King Cobra," I ordered. I was trying to sound confident, as if this were a weekly routine. *It's Friday. Time to pick up the ol' case of King Cobra!* The clerk wordlessly walked to the refrigerated coolers and retrieved my order. I gave him the money, my hands shaking like tiny earthquakes. He passed me dollar bills, assorted coinage, and my malt liquor, two very different kinds of change.

In a made-up film version of my life, this moment might dispatch me down a narratively convenient path. "Surely," I'd say, staring deeply into a half-empty bottle, disgust painting my face, "there must be a beer that doesn't taste like liquid nails." And then I'd depart on a lifelong pursuit of better-tasting beer, seeking IPAs and stouts in abandoned warehouses, dim garages, and the industrial hinterlands of cities decimated by postindustrial decline. Or maybe I'd protest malt liquor's questionable advertising tactics, starting a crusade to spread the sordid tale about how breweries first peddled the strong beer to the aspirational white middle class as an upper-crust beverage (hello, Country Club!), later using hip-hop to court the urban and minority demographic.

Reality is rarely wrapped with a tidy bow. We bought King Cobra because my friends and I wanted to sit by campfires and catch a buzz and conversation, plain and simple. Taste sat a distant second to beer's function as fun fuel burning bright in the dark night, with no worries of what we'd feel like in the morning.

In truth, my beer story would make for a great commercial advertising repetition. Night after night,

adult me began paying attention to flavor and aroma, mentally categorizing the differences between sweetly muscular English barley wines and Germany's elegantly fruity kölsch. No beer sensei guided me to a state of fermented enlightenment. I just drank lots and lots of beer and paid lots and lots of attention. I also asked questions of brewers, bartenders, sales reps, brewery owners, fellow drinkers—anyone and everyone with more beer smarts than me, which was anyone and everyone.

Two decades later, I still haven't stopped drinking beer or inquiring why. It's a journalist's inquisitive duty. I call people and ask for opinions, advice, and distinct viewpoints, later distilled into stories that unfurl larger truths about light lagers or the latest trend in beer.

And there's always another trend.

Always another reason to ask experts for assistance.

THE WISDOM OF THE BEER-DRINKING CROWDS

Notice I said *experts*, not *expert*. There's never one person standing atop Mount Knowledge, doling out bits and pieces of beer brilliance. The brewing industry is an eight-hundred-armed octopus, tentacles working in concert to deliver great-tasting beer to your hand.

Some are easy to identify. Visibly, brewers are responsible for mixing grain with hot water and some appealingly smelly flowers, and then giving yeast a forever home. But let's not forget about the rarely seen

El Bait Shop, in Des Moines, Iowa, has 262 taps of draft beer.

draft-line techs helping bars pour squeaky-clean pints, or the scientists sitting in labs ensuring that beer possesses the right kind of contagion and carbonation. What advice could they impart to drinkers trying to better navigate the increasingly confusing world of beer?

My second book, *Complete Beer Course*, came out in 2013. Some three thousand breweries operated in America around then, and my goal was to orient beer on a living historical continuum. Here's how the past colors our present, styles and approaches coming in and out of fashion as easily as acid-washed jeans and combat boots. Drink a selection of time-honored Belgian, German, and English ales and lagers, complement that with modern IPAs and imperial stouts, and—cue the flashing lights—you'd earn a solid educational foundation.

That seems like sixty-five million years ago, an era when dinosaurs and flagship beers ruled the earth.

The country's brewery count has more than doubled and is inching toward a number I don't dare write. It'll fast be as obsolete as the trails leading drinkers deep into the beer world. Belgian monks' rich dubbels and strong and fruity tripels now occupy side roads. IPAs clog the interstates of introduction, on-ramps occupied by hazy beers as soft and fruity as pillows made of ripe peaches. New beers debut so swiftly that police officers could clock releases with a speed gun. Sugary pastry stouts now evoke cookies, cake, and candy bars, syrupy extravagances that could very well cause hangovers *and* cavities.

Beer now is like those college friends who spent a semester abroad and returned home with new quirks, clothes, and opinions. They're the same people, sure,

Adding beer to barrels for aging.

but they've changed. I write about beer professionally and I'm confused. Maybe you are too. To explain our fast-evolving beer ecosystem, I decided to tap the brains of some of beer's most brilliant thinkers across the industry's full spectrum: brewers, sensory experts, label designers, beer buyers, Master Cicerones, bottle-shop owners, chefs, food-pairing savants, and international judges—more than one hundred people in total, their wisdom collected, digested, and shaped into *Drink Better Beer*.

Throughout the project, I learned that I have so much more to learn about beer. I discovered the telltale clues that bars and shops care about beer quality, as well as how Michelin-starred brewpubs are deftly updating beer and food pairings. I traveled to Allagash

Brewing to sit through the company's rigorous sensory panels, and learned that creating consistent beer is a choreographed team effort. A professor schooled me with scientific discoveries that IPAs can, in fact, contain too many hops, while another academic offered a fresh outlook on beer appreciation by removing eyesight from appraisals. I asked beer writers and brewery owners to reveal their essential beer destinations, while others shared their brewed awakenings—the moments when beer flips from bubbly drunk water into a sophisticated beverage that delivers pleasures and demands deep analysis, the catalyst for boundless investigation and creation, beer as both muse and career.

We're not holding back any secrets. Here's how to drink better beer.

WHAT'S IN STORE

BUYING BEER IN THE MODERN MARKETPLACE

Buying snacks once required more mental calculus than purchasing beer. Maybe some crunchy cheese puffs? What about the barbecue-flavored potato chips? Those Doritos sure look delicious, but do you want Nacho Cheese or Cool Ranch? Or would you be happier with tortilla chips and one of those thirty-two brands of salsa? Decisions, decisions, decisions. Beer was easy. You bought the same lager as last week, or the similar one on sale, preferably in bulk just like toilet paper. Don't want to run out!

These days, beer commerce is a mite bit more complicated. Beers of every conceivable, and inconceivable, formulation and strength besiege grocery, liquor, and specialty stores. They're bazaars of flavor, some familiar, some just bizarre. Picking between a chocolate peanut butter stout, a New England IPA, and a refreshing pilsner can be dizzying, afflicting folks with what I like to call wine-store syndrome, or buying based on little more than labels and leaps of faith.

Hazy IPAs sit on the bar at San Francisco's City Beer Store.

Look, I'm a sucker for stellar branding—all the better to artfully Instagram in an outstretched hand. And basing purchases on looks isn't an altogether awful plan. Great designs and great beers often go hand in hand, and for good reason. Today's best beers will appeal to eyes and palates alike, and breweries need to win over both to create that winning equation.

Still, there are smarter ways to buy an IPA. The beer industry's continued evolution has created new pathways and customs of buying beer. Today, customers can drink electrifyingly fresh beer at brewery taprooms in the afternoon, then return at dawn to queue for cases of just-canned double IPA. The glass growler's hold on draft beer has been shattered by the aluminum Crowler, part of brewing's bear hug of cans, cylinders of intense buyer desire.

Specialty beer stores are also boosting their game. No longer is stocking any available hop water enough. The best shops handpick inventory as fastidiously as art museums curate exhibitions, and quality is always prized over quantity. Ranks of savvy clerks help customers smartly fill shopping carts, and maybe give them a reason to linger over a Belgian lambic at the on-premise bar. There's simply too much great beer brewed around the world to waste a sliver of sobriety on a stout evocative of rusty pennies, headaches, and regret. We all have a limited number of liver tokens allotted for each day. Here's how to spend them wisely.

Some of the thousand-plus beers at Belmont Station in Portland, Oregon, one of the country's best bottle shops.

MAKE SURE COOLERS ARE CURATED

I came of cultural age in the '90s and spent much of my discretionary teenage income—earned refereeing soccer games and deep frying chicken tenders at Burger King—on concerts and CDs. As an alternateen favoring Manic Panic hair dye and flannel, I avoided Camelot Music, National Record Mart, and other relics of mall culture. Instead, I patronized independent record shops, sonic repositories that catered to left-of-the-dial tastes.

Two decades later, in an age of cold computer algorithms and tech-curated recommendations, I seek similarly curated experiences in beer stores.

Yeah, I'll toss the odd twelve-pack into my cart during the weekly grocery run, but I generally avoid large-scale alcohol depots where beer cases are stacked six feet high and dust bunnies prowl concrete floors. Abundance may be impressive at first, like a sprawling Vegas buffet laden with fried shrimp, prime rib, and an array of chocolate cakes, but not everything is going to be fresh. Moreover, the human body has a finite capacity for consumption. We're not all built like Joey Chestnut, the competitive eater who once devoured seventy-four hot dogs, or Wade Boggs, the former Boston Red Sox baseball player who admitted to consuming 107 beers during one notable drinking jag. (One hundred! And seven! Beers!)

Less can be so much more. All I want is a couple of nice beers to take me through the evening, something fresh and carefully vetted by someone I can trust. "People always laugh when I say, 'Don't worry, we drink shitty beer, so you don't have to,'" says Suzanne Schalow, the cofounder of the Craft Beer Cellar family of more than thirty national stores.

The role of beer-store owners is changing. They've gone from hunters to gatekeepers. "From a buyer's perspective, it used to be your responsibility to source new beers, find styles that people had never heard of, and find ways to display them and educate," says Craig Wathen, who owns San Francisco's City Beer Store with his wife, Beth. The couple opened City Beer in 2006, a much more hands-on era of selling beer. Back then, the couple spent many, many minutes explaining concepts such as, yes, that beer really should be sour. A decade later, both education and retail have evolved, so much so that Germany's tart and salty gose, a style that was essentially extinct, is now

---

★ ★ ★

Fun Fact: During one particularly memorable episode of *It's Always Sunny in Philadelphia*, a darkly comic TV show about drunks who run a bar, the gang attempts to best Wade Boggs's record by drinking some seventy beers on a cross-country flight. Spoiler alert: it does not go well.

★ ★ ★

---

sold in supermarket cold cases. Paucity has become abundance, leading to shifting responsibilities.

"There are so many suppliers and options, it's more about culling the herd," Craig says. "As a buyer, I'm making sure what gets into the shop is the best that's out there. It's a little different mentality when you put your hat on and go to work."

LISTEN FOR CHATTER, NOT THE TELEVISION

These highly discerning beer stores are also evolving into a unique hybrid of commerce and community pub. Thanks to licenses that allow many stores to sell beer to stay and to go, customers can pop in for a pint and leave with a clutch of bottles and cans.

Belmont Station, in Portland, Oregon, is a bottle shop with an adjoining bar, the Biercafé, offering thirty-four rotating drafts plus fresh cask ale. "People are able to take their draft beer and go shopping," says managing partner Lisa Morrison. The Beer Temple, in Chicago, is a combo bottle shop and taproom dispensing twenty drafts at their ideal serving temperature. Seattle's sunny and communal TeKu Tavern offers more than fifty taps organized by flavor profiles and a wall of fridges filled with beer for consumption on or off the premises.

In Brooklyn, I regularly visit Covenhoven to sip one of the sixteen rotating drafts, such as Suarez Family Brewery's unfiltered Palatine Pils (see pages 30–31), while perusing coolers as I once did racks of records and CDs, seeking something cold, something new, often soliciting input from fellow shoppers. I

Author Joshua M. Bernstein at Brooklyn's Covenhoven, which partners sixteen taps with fridges full of beers and ciders to stay or go.

crave human connection even more than I do the next mega-hopped this or that. Beer builds conversational bridges like no other beverage.

"You can turn to a perfect stranger and start talking about beer, and before you know it you're sharing a bottle," says Beth Wathen of City Beer Store. "That community component is essential to the bottle shop experience." The Wathens' slightly subterranean store fast became a gathering place where folks could congregate over rounds of California IPAs. Customers regularly left City Beer, which expanded in 2018 to

a larger location, with new beers and friends. The focus here is on humans and alcohol, not televisions broadcasting the nightly sporting event. "Purposely, we don't have televisions in our space because we want to encourage that interaction," Beth says. "You're almost forced to talk to the person next to you because you don't have a big screen to look at."

It's funny what happens when you look up from your phone. I'm as prone as any other twenty-first-century human to idly scroll social media. But as I often tell people, beer makes us chatty for a reason.

That porter-boosted banter can lead to a different kind of social interaction. "Having the bar side allows people to taste samples, and that opens up a whole new world," Beth says.

Not too far back at City Beer, a gaggle of friends were sipping a gently acidic selection from Portland, Oregon's Cascade Brewing, one of the country's best pucker producers. "They got really excited about it and went straight to the bottle shop and were like, I just had this amazing Rose City Sour," Beth says of Cascade's wine barrel–aged creation that's infused with rose petals and hips. "What is something else similar?

Suddenly you saw another person point something out and say, I had one of these the other day and it was really good. Next thing you know, there was gathering of eight people drinking sour beers, and half of them didn't previously know each other."

The couple also uses conversation to guide customers to their ideal beer. "I think the most important thing is not so much asking, 'What kind of beer do you drink?' It's more about, 'What kind of flavors do you like in your beverages and what do you like to eat?'" Beth says. "Then we can go into different styles and not talk so much about beer names specifically."

> **BREWED AWAKENING:** "I was a lager drinker throughout university, but while working in South Korea I tasted the beer that literally changed my life. In response to the lackluster lagers on offer, my now-husband and I decided to look up the local homebrewing club. In a city of some 10 million it so happened that the guy who ran the homebrew club lived in our building! On first meeting we tasted his signature beer, a double IPA called 'Death By Hops.' After that first sip, I felt like every beer I'd had up to that point had been a waste! I'll be forever grateful to the brewer, Rob Titley, for starting me on a beer appreciation journey that has become a passion, a profession, and if I'm honest, an obsession."
>
> —Lucy Corne, South African beer and travel writer, author of *Beer Safari*

★ ★ ★

Advice: When I help people select a beer, I often hear this sentence: "I don't like beers that are too hoppy." After gentle prodding, I discover that's not what they mean. They dislike beers that are too *bitter*. It's OK to hate bitterness! It's divisive. A bitter beer can have loads of hops, but *hoppy* is not a synonym for *bitter*.

★ ★ ★

CHECK WHETHER STORES ARE COOL

Sometimes when I walk into a really good beer store, I wonder why I'm so cold. Should I have brought a sweatshirt to warm my bones? A slightly cooler environment, right around the temperature of a sunny

The IPAs are kept properly cold at Belmont Station in Portland, Oregon.

northeastern fall afternoon, is a chilly reminder that a shop really cares about its precious cargo.

"We're at 65 degrees [Fahrenheit] year-round," says Craft Beer Cellar's Schalow. "Beer is fermented cold and should be cold its entire life. People look at me and say, 'No wonder you keep it freezing in here.' I tell them, 'If we were as cool as we should be, it would be 48 degrees in here.'"

This is backed up by science. In 1889, Swedish scientist Svante Arrhenius—he later won a Nobel Prize for chemistry—put forth a formula concerning temperature's impact on chemical reactions. Essentially, the reaction rate doubles for every increase of ten degrees Celsius (eighteen degrees Fahrenheit) in temperature. Know how you're more active when the weather warms up? Molecules are much the same. Increased activity amplifies oxygen's opportunity to wreak havoc, interacting with compounds and accelerating the process of oxidation. It's why beer can taste dull, stale, and not unlike puréed cardboard.

Breweries do their best to minimize oxygen pickup during packaging, but a little O2 will always infiltrate beer. The molecule's destructive rampage may be inevitable, but it can be slowed by cold. "Refrigeration extends life," Schalow says. Which is a fine segue to a question I'm commonly asked: Will my beer go bad if it warms up? Nope. Beer is not like a mayonnaise-slicked macaroni salad, developing unwanted pathogens if it sits warm for too long. (It always will. Nobody wants macaroni salad at a picnic.) What you want to avoid is leaving beer in a locked car during a broiling heat wave, windows rolled tight. "You're going to create a cooking environment," Schalow explains.

It's helpful to think of beer as you do fruit and vegetables, sturdy yet perishable, best when stored cool and out of the sunlight. "We're constantly telling people, 'Treat beer like lettuce,'" Schalow says. "Lettuce is also going to be fine for three hours. You can take a beer from a fridge, put it in your car for two or three hours, and it's going to be just fine."

DON'T SEE THE LIGHT

There are other significant tells that your local store takes extra steps to care for beer, starting with shielding bottles from ultraviolet rays. Whether from sunshine or incandescent light bulbs, ultraviolet rays interact with hops' alpha acids (they lend bitterness) to create 3-methyl-2-butene-thiol. In layman's terms, it's

Since 2006, San Francisco's City Beer Store has operated as a combination bar and bottle shop.

Lisa Morrison is the managing partner at Belmont Station in Portland, Oregon.

Morrison, whose store was founded in 1997 and remains a trusted destination for Pacific Northwest drinkers. Belmont offers more than 1,400 vetted selections, ranging from Portland standouts such as Wayfinder, Breakside, and Ex Novo to Belgian mainstays such as Westmalle and De Ranke. The beers are tidily arranged and the labels faced forward, both positive tells. "One of the things that I think proves that the staff in that bottle shop is really laying hands on beers is that all the beers are faced on the shelves," Morrison says. "That means the staff is on their game."

Speaking to staff is also a cheat code for figuring out the best and freshest beer. "I can guarantee you that anybody who works in a beer store or a beer bar is going to love to talk about what they like to drink right now," says Morrison. "Not only does it get you a pretty good beer, but it also opens up the possibility of more conversation down the road."

NICE PACKAGE: THE RISE OF CANS, CROWLERS, AND NEW WAYS OF SELLING BEER

A decade ago, maybe longer, I spent a ski weekend in Colorado, at the mouth of Rocky Mountain National Park. To stock the fridge, my friends drove to Oskar Blues' nearby brewpub and bought cases of Dale's Pale Ale. To us, 12 ounces of canned, well-bittered pale ale felt like a radical's firebomb, rule breaking and revolutionary.

a stinky compound that's also present in skunk spray. Don't want your beer to smell like a camping disaster? Speed-walk from any shop that displays beer, especially bottles, in sunny windows. It's a million-watt advertisement for a dearth of knowledge about caring for beer.

"Our windows have a UV-protected film and all of our lights are UV-filtered," says Belmont Station's

Advice: Brewers devise and package beer to the best of their abilities, then distributors port liquid from A to B. The process takes time. You can curse scientists for their inability to develop a teleportation device, but until then we live in a reality where it takes a week or two to truck beer across America or cruise bottles across a body of water. "It takes five days for our beer to reach the East Coast," says Patrick Rue, the founder of California's the Bruery. "Generally, the earliest we can get it is six to seven days after packaging."

Craig and Beth Wathen are co-owners of San Francisco's City Beer Store.

Nowadays the outcast—first canned in 2002—is the norm. Supermarkets stock twelve-packs of Sierra Nevada Pale Ale and Brooklyn Lager cans, and aluminum-jacketed double IPAs like the Alchemist's Heady Topper and Tree House's Bright are fetishized. "It helped even the staunchest beer geek realize that it was not the vessel it came in, but it was the beer that mattered," says Russ Phillips, author of *Canned: Artwork of the Modern American Beer Can.*

During the early days of George W. Bush's presidency, canned beer meant lagers bought cold, cheap, and in quantities vast enough to fill a kiddie pool. Now public perception has done an about-face. Outdated tropes of tinny taste have vanished, as today's cans keep beer fresher for longer, ably vanquishing bottled beers' mortal enemies, oxygen and sunlight.

If You Build It, They Will Can

Be it soda or beer, the canning business was built on economies of scale, pumping out truckloads of product and passing on the savings to customers. While this model works for Coca-Cola and brewing conglomerates, smaller brewers typically lack the liquid volume or capital. Costs of high-speed automated machines can easily top $100,000, and even entry-level canners can still cost more than $15,000.

Affordable, small-batch canning was once as mythical as single-payer health care. Boulder's Jeff Aldred helped make it real. "We'll go in there with our magic sword and get your problem solved," jokes Aldred, a cofounder of Wild Goose Canning. The

Iron Heart Canning travels to breweries to can their beer.

firm started as a systems integrator, creating computing systems that combine hardware and software. In fall 2008, Wild Goose's neighbor, Upslope Brewing, enlisted Wild Goose to upgrade its canning line. It became the prototype for the faster, more efficient Micro-Can system.

The modular, space-saving unit was a sensation, turning Wild Goose into breweries' go-to canning fabricator. (Cask Brewing Systems and Process and Packaging Machine Corporation are other important players.) To date, the company has sold hundreds of systems to the likes of La Cumbre, AleSmith, and Fair State Brewing Cooperative, plus wineries, cideries, distilleries, and coffee roasters. "Depending how big you are, we have a machine that will fit your needs," Aldred says.

At the request of several budding businesspeople, Wild Goose solved the riddle of creating a portable canning unit that was easy to assemble, disassemble, and transport, and that wouldn't rattle apart on the road. By fall 2011, Mobile Canning Colorado was

HOW TO READ A BEER LABEL

Every label tells a story about the liquid. Here's your handy
cheat sheet to a label's most common acronyms.

★ ★ ★

(A) Name: The brewing industry will never run dry on puns.

(B) Tagline: Marketing speak designed to impart a brand's desired vibe or personality.

(C) SRM: The Standard Reference Method is used to measure a beer's color. A straw-pale pilsner will measure 2, while a pitch-black imperial stout will be north of 40.

(D) IBU: The international bitterness units scale is a measure of a beer's perceived bitterness. Generally speaking, the lower the number, the less bitter a beer will be. IBUs don't exist in a vacuum, and a beer's strength, acidity, and sweetness play a big role in how you register bitterness.

(E) ABV: Alcohol by volume measures, duh, the amount of alcohol in a beverage. For example, lagers hover around 5 percent ABV, while double IPAs hit 8 percent ABV or higher. Do basic math to monitor your intake. To wit: A 10 percent triple IPA isn't just 3 percent more potent than a 7 percent IPA. It's more than 50 *percent* stronger.

(F) Yeast: Most beers utilize either ale or lager strains. The words *wild* or *Brett* signify a beer fermented with *Brettanomyces*, an unruly strain that can create earthy, rustic, or even tropical aromatics.

in business, and the era of itinerant canning was afoot. Armed with Wild Goose equipment, scores of nomadic canneries now roam the roads, packaging beer wherever required. "When craft brewers are starting to get into packaging, they're overwhelmingly choosing cans," says Jared Brody of can manufacturer Ball Corporation.

> **BREWED AWAKENING:** "Pete's Wicked Ale was the first beer to slap me upside the head and force me to explore the idea of more complex beer. In the late '80s and early '90s, we used to drive a couple hundred miles from Alabama to Atlanta just to get our hands on it."
>
> —Dale Katechis, founder, Oskar Blues Brewery

Bombs Away: The Fast Fade of 22-Ounce Bottles

For most of this millennium, the dominant delivery vehicle for specialty and one-off beers was the 22-ounce glass bottle. Bombers, as they're commonly called, offered consumers a chance to try new beers at somewhat affordable prices. I used to pretty much exclusively buy bombers of IPAs such as Lagunitas Hop Stoopid and Bear Republic Racer 5, getting to know beers over the course of a 22-ounce courtship. Drinkers today have ghosted that technique. "Whether you like the 22-ounce IPA or not, I can tell you that it just doesn't sell," says City Beer Store's Craig Wathen.

The bomber is destined for the great recycling bin in the sky, and a huge reason is mobile canning. In 2013, when Tyler Wille founded Iron Heart Canning in Monroe, Connecticut, canned craft beer was a relative rarity. "It was a barren landscape," he says. "Bombers were king." Over the ensuing years, Wille watched his company grow—Iron Heart now operates from Maine to Florida, and as far west as Ohio, Kentucky, and Tennessee—and packaging preferences shift. "The industry has done a complete 180," he says. "The package that was predominantly the specialty package is now nearly out of existence."

Iron Heart and fellow mobile canners gave breweries of all scales the ability to put their beers in cans, a small uprising on its own. "It's not just big breweries that can afford a production-level canning line; it's any and every brewery under the sun," he says.

How forgotten are bombers? We couldn't find a picture of 22-ounce bottles, so we went with this shot from a German beer store.

The Eyes Have It

The rise of cans represented another kind of insurgency. Breweries such as Boston's Trillium and Los Angeles's Monkish began producing hazy IPAs with heightened aromatics and scant bitterness, packaged in 16-ounce cans bedazzled with eye-catching labels. Whereas once I fawned over album art, analyzing liner notes with Talmudic intensity, now I cradled 16-ounce cans and sought words that would bring me joy: Mosaic and Citra, the fruity, tropical hops that set IPAs on a juicy new course.

"You can't interact with a piece of brand messaging more intimately than a can," says Christian Helms, owner and creative director of Helms Workshop. His Austin-based design firm has created the visual language for breweries including Fullsteam, Bauhaus Brew Labs, and Modern Times Beer. He says of the can, "It's a blank slate that you can wrap 360 degrees."

Chicago's Half Acre is a great example of a brewery that embraces the graphic potential of a can. The brewery employs a few designers to dream up visually charged designs such as GoneAway IPA's snake-and-cactus southwestern vibe and Pony Pilsner's gloriously maned horse. "Design is a gateway to introducing your beer to someone," says founder Gabriel Magliaro. He notes that while top-notch beer is essential, graphics paint a broader picture of a brewery's identity. "If the design is good and the beer is good, you have a pretty good chance of drawing in a fan," he says.

Breweries today use the can as a canvas for eye-catching artwork.

MASSIVE BEERS, MINISCULE PACKAGES

★ ★ ★

I spend most days working in my apartment, alone except for the scores of oversize barley wine and imperial stout bottles lining my office's shelves, floor, and closet, the wax caps and champagne corks growing dustier every day. And I rarely have a bad enough one to drink 22 ounces of a 15 percent stout by myself. I'm not alone. "We saw the shrinking world of bombers," says Josh Deth, the founder of Chicago's Revolution Brewing. In 2017, the brewery stopped packaging beers like its barrel-aged Deth's Tar imperial oatmeal stout in bombers, moving to 12-ounce cans, a more responsible serving size, a beer I'd happily sip on a weeknight. Industry-wide, breweries such as Odell and Southern Tier have switched stronger beers to smaller, 12-ounce bottles, while Indiana's Flat12

Bierwerks favors stubby 8-ounce cans, the kind used by the soft-drink industry, for its imperial stout Pinko! Notably, the 8-ounce can is becoming a favored format for breweries packaging beers of potencies big and small. Workhorse Brewing, near Philadelphia, puts New England IPAs and pilsners alike in the mini package, while Chicago's Hopewell Brewing sells Lil Buddy. It's a low-alcohol helles lager that's equally compelling and crushable, so cute you feel bad crumpling an empty can.

"Sometimes we just want to drink a little bit less, and that means both quantity and the actual style." says cofounder Samantha Lee. "We're providing a different way to drink beer."

You won't find Lil Buddy loitering in my office. Because I drank every last one.

Hopewell Brewing only sells its Lil Buddy lager in 8-ounce cans.

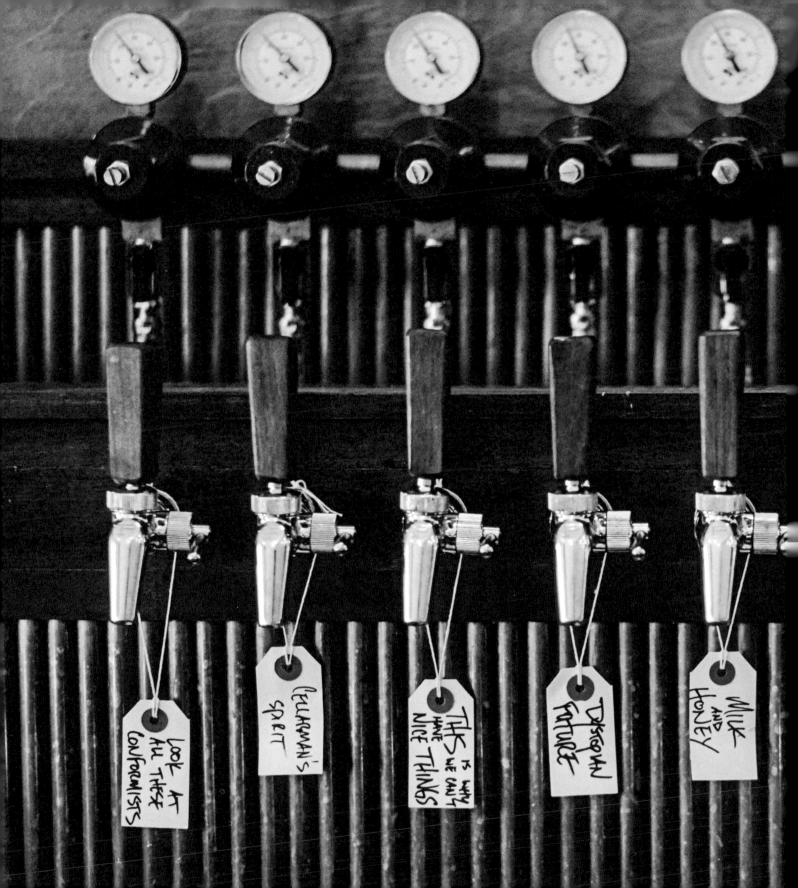

DR. TOM SHELLHAMMER

Nor'Wester Endowed Professor of Brewing Science at Oregon State University

★ ★ ★

Dr. Tom Shellhammer is one of America's preeminent hop experts.

In 2001, Oregon State University hired Dr. Tom Shellhammer to research beer chemistry, a field tailored to his interests and strengths. He earned a degree in fermentation science from the University of California, Davis, home to one of America's preeminent brewing programs, followed by a master's in food science and a PhD in food engineering.

Beer chemistry is a big arena. Dr. Shellhammer needed a niche. "When I first came to Oregon State, I'm looking around like, 'Where am I going to be able find money to work in an area that I'm interested in and have the skills in?'" he says. What about hops? OSU has long operated a hops breeding program with the USDA, so studying them felt like a fitting discipline. He developed a few ideas. He found funding. And thus his calling as one of the world's preeminent experts on hops' aromas, flavors, and mysteries, an apt person to discuss American beer's contemporary excesses.

Forty years back, hop bitterness balanced malt sweetness. Now, brewers shower beers with hops to deliver hurricane-strength gusts of fragrance and flavor. "We're not really a culture of finesse," says Dr. Shellhammer, now OSU's Nor'Wester Endowed Professor of Brewing Science. "If one pound of hops per barrel is enough, let's do two pounds of hops. I'll show you, I'll do 10 pounds

a barrel. Just keep putting more and more material in there."

The extravagance is mostly earmarked for dry-hopping, during which hops are added postfermentation to impart colossal scents and minute bitterness. "People often called hops the spice of beer because they were used in such small amounts," Dr. Shellhammer says. "Now brewers are almost making hop teas or hop infusions."

IPAs are regularly double, triple, and even quadruple dry-hopped. More flavor. More aroma. More . . . what is that? "You can get upward of one-third of the total dry matter of the hops extracted into the beer," Dr. Shellhammer says. "Hops have sugars, proteins, and minerals, and at these high levels they can have a transformative effect."

Certain hops possess enzymes that can break down nonfermentable sugars into fermentable sugars. Lingering yeast will restart fermentation and elevate alcohol and carbonation, potentially leading to off flavors such as diacetyl. Pass the butterscotch candies, please. Time to meet "hop creep."

"You're putting plant material into beers at relatively high levels and relatively cool conditions. If there were any residual enzyme activity, it wouldn't be surprising if it could have a significant effect on beer," Dr. Shellhammer says. "When I first bumped into this it was surprising, but now it's like, 'Of course.'"

Brewers and scientists can measure a hop's bitter precursors—alpha acids—and quantify them in a finished beer. Those are bitterness units, the BUs in IBUs. They're a pretty decent prediction of a beer's bitterness intensity. "The caveat is that bitterness is not a good predictor of aromatic intensity," Dr. Shellhammer says.

Conventional wisdom would go like this: the greater a hop variety's essential oils (their compounds are responsible for fragrance and flavor), the greater the aroma. But that's not always correct. Neither is adding additional hops. "Just how efficient is this process when you dry-hop? How much are you actually getting out of the hops? It looks to be remarkably inefficient," he says.

Hops are not an infinite resource, flowing as freely as water from a summertime sprinkler. They're an agrarian product governed by Mother Nature's fickle whims. It's easy to use mounds of hops when the going is good, but the going is rarely good forever. Breweries will need to adapt, and that's where hop researchers can supply a crucial assist.

Recently, Dr. Shellhammer was attending a meeting of the annual Craft Brewers Conference when he bumped into a former student who'd listened to his lectures. "Out of the blue he said, 'You know, Tom, the stuff you're studying in terms of hop creep and bitterness is totally changing the way I brew beer,'" Dr. Shellhammer recalls. "I didn't set out to do work to try to change the way people brew beer. To have that validation was cool."

Brewers will never stop experimenting with hops. New varieties will keep appearing every year, and there will always be new opportunities for research for Dr. Shellhammer's lab. (You bet the laboratory is looking into the biotransformations you will read on pages 34–35.) The tiny green cones contain endless puzzles, a lifetime of inquisition that feels like neither bore nor chore. "I'm doing work on beer. I love beer. It's a cool thing to study," he says. "Stuff I'm working on is stuff you can smell, taste, and see."

★ ★ ★

Advice: "The fact that we have more than 7,000 breweries now, from a statistical perspective and the fact that not everybody in the industry knows what they are doing, your odds of finding poor or defective beer now have never been greater. Some consumers will find more poorly constructed, mediocre, or off beer now than when we had fewer breweries."

—Dr. Tom Shellhammer

★ ★ ★

BREWING AND DIVERSITY: A WORK IN PROGRESS

★ ★ ★

To me, brewery taprooms are as comfy as my trusty red sweatshirt. It's easy for me to be at ease in taprooms because, to be blunt, I'm a glasses-wearing white dude—brewpubs and taprooms are the natural habitats of beer-loving people like me.

"Craft brewers didn't really target black and brown people," says Kevin Bradford, a partner in New York City's Harlem Hops. "It's a market that was overlooked." But slowly, American breweries are venturing outside the usual lines and making diversity and inclusion key pillars of their businesses.

The Medium Is the Message

Originally under the Dope & Dank banner, Teo Hunter and Beny Ashburn introduced people of color to aromatic hazy IPAs and snappy pilsners by curating events at barbershops and sneaker stores. "The community of black and brown people was a missing element," Hunter says of contemporary beer culture.

The Los Angeles twosome made T-shirts proclaiming black and brown people love beer, the message a rallying call to create kinship. "When we created our shirts, it was initially a beacon to say, 'Hey, we're here. If you're out there and appreciate beer the way we do, now you know you're not alone,'" Hunter says.

Ultimately, Hunter and Ashburn realized their mission would be more impactful on their own terms, on their own turf. "Asking for permission and asking for that opportunity to have a presence got tiring," Hunter says.

In 2020, the duo plan to open Crowns & Hops, a brewery and taproom in Inglewood, a heavily Hispanic and African-American neighborhood in Los Angeles. "We want to reintroduce the model of what it means to enjoy an alcoholic beverage with your family, in a place where your kids can eat, and you can bring your dog," he says. "These elements have been void in our communities."

Beny Ashburn and Teo Hunter of Crowns & Hops.

Members of the Border X team.

Border Crossing

Perhaps America's hottest-button issue right now is its southern border, where the debate is whether to be open, walled off, or somewhere in between. "It feels important to stand up and say, 'No, we love the border. We love the mixing,'" says David Favela, the CEO of Border X Brewing, a family run brewery with several California locations.

Border X was born in fall 2013, in San Diego, one mile from the Mexican border, the beers drawing inspiration from the other side of the fence. The popular Mexican drink agua de Jamaica, made with hibiscus flowers, inspired Blood Saison, while Abuelita's Chocolate Stout starred cinnamon-y Mexican chocolate. The taproom's nightly event calendar contains events such as a lively *lotería*, a Mexican bingo-like game of chance, as well as weekly Latin music jams. "We get retired bankers, people from the neighborhood, and motorcycle clubs with their leather cuts on," Favela says. "It's not only mixes of ages, but mixes from different walks of life."

In 2019, Border X expanded to Bell, a suburb of Los Angeles with a large Latino community. "Our target market is Latinos," Favela says. "We start with them, rather than making them an afterthought."

The Price Is Right

"In communities I talked to, pricing was a major issue," says Sergio Manancero, the president and taproom manager of La Doña Brewing, in Minneapolis, Minnesota. So La Doña's Mexican lager, Doña Fria, sells for a fiver.

La Doña is the rare brewery registered as a public benefit corporation—basically, a socially minded for-profit business. Its mastermind is Manancero, the son of Uruguayan immigrants and a Marine veteran who returned to Minneapolis in 2013 after several tours of duty in Afghanistan and discovered a thriving brewing scene, one sorely lacking people that looked liked him.

Vibrant skull murals cover the walls at La Doña, and there's regular salsa dancing, as well as soccer matches in a boxed-in turf field designed for three-on-three contests. "Soccer represents a more worldly culture than any other sport, especially in Latin America where everything is about soccer," he says. "There are so many different ways to display culture and invite people in."

As breweries grow ever more diverse, taprooms can become crucial rendezvous points for people of every persuasion, all of us finding common ground while clinking beers as varied as the crowd itself.

Tapping a New Business Model

The ascension of cans coincided with the beer industry's other major shift, the taproom. No longer were drinkers discovering beers on shelves. They were traveling to the source to drink and buy beer brewed and packaged just steps from where they stood, in old warehouses and factories in their hometowns. Beer wasn't just some liquid that magically flowed from a faucet; it was a beverage brewed by your coworker's friend, the one who always homebrewed in the garage. "Consumers want to go to a brewery and buy beer at the brewery," Wille says.

Drinking at brewery taprooms now accounts for around 10 percent of volume and is growing, according to the Brewers Association. The new class of customer-facing breweries sells beer on tap and to go, predominantly in cans packaged by the breweries

A view of the brewery at Brooklyn's Circa Brewing.

Customers queue to buy cans of beer at Brooklyn's Other Half Brewing.

themselves or by mobile canning companies like Iron Heart. This new way of getting new beer struck a consumer chord, reverberating across America. "The consumer base shifted extraordinarily quickly to wanting four-packs of 16-ounce cans," Wille says. "That is the package that everybody is flocking to and lining up for."

Wait, Wait: Let Me Tell You about Lines

The haze craze has led to some peculiar behavior. Like an alternate-universe Black Friday, the rabid shopping holiday following Thanksgiving, beer fans started lining up before sunrise at breweries like Tired Hands, outside Philadelphia, and Brooklyn's Other Half to buy the latest experiment in hop expression. Why? We're humans. We like waiting for sneakers, smartphones, cronuts, and burgers encased in ramen. The underlying mesh uniting this mixture of mania and patience is FOMO—fear of missing out.

Since you're reading this book, here's my $24.95* worth of advice: If you want to stand in a column of humanity and wait for beer, tally ho! Good things come to those who wait, or so I've heard. Personally,

*I wish! Does anyone actually pay full price for books?

I liken beer lines to spending hours queuing for a brunch table: There are plenty of pancakes and eggs available everywhere. Why wait?

Crowler Power

I used to have a really great collection of growlers, enough to line a couple of shelves in my cupboard and make my wife wonder, "Why do you have so many growlers?" Answer: because they're growlers! The glass jugs were my companions whenever I'd hit breweries or beer stores like Brooklyn's dearly departed Bierkraft, where I'd fill my growlers with 64 fluid ounces of bubbly goodness. Growlers were how I brought home fresh beer, emphasis on *were*.

Today, I have options for bringing home brewery-fresh beer, most notably the Crowler. The canned growler's conception traces to Oskar Blues, where the brewery's production manager was tinkering with a vintage tabletop canner, the sort used to seal tomatoes in steel cans. The realization that the contraption could be modified to fit 32-ounce cans from the Ball Corporation spawned a partnership between the two companies and the wide release of a device for canning draft beer in a single-use, lightweight, sunlight-proof, and recyclable package that's guaranteed clean.

No matter whether you're Team Glass or Team Can, there are a few things to know about your preferred packaging. Growlers are typically filled straight from taps, a process that's a little less hygienic than you might like. "The faucets are sometimes submerged in beer, creating a breeding ground for line infection—mmm, sour butter—so some breweries will attach a length of plastic hose to fill a growler, [to] push out foam and to be more sanitary," says Em Sauter, the author of *Beer Is for Everyone (of Drinking Age)*.

Moreover, the process introduces beer's mortal enemy, oxygen, destroyer of freshness, bringer of staleness. Once growlers are uncapped, additional oxygen skedaddles inside and carbonation makes a jail break, never to return. Beer's irreversible journey to stillness has begun.

Ideally, you'll want to finish an opened growler that day, the next one tops. Think of growlers as takeout containers for perishable liquid goods, best consumed on the double. You don't wait a week to eat that delivery

Em Sauter is the author of *Beer Is for Everyone (of Drinking Age)*.

lo mein, right? And when you're done with a growler, remember to do the dishes. "Make sure after you drink it that you rinse it with very hot water (skip the dishwasher or soap, which can taint future fillings) and let it air-dry," Sauter says. "This will keep your growler happy."

Crowlers, though, are only as good as a brewery's staff. Before filling empty cans, workers should purge oxygen with CO2. This will extend a beer's life-span, though no beer is immortal. "Not filling it properly can lead to some sadness, and I have experienced said sadness," Sauter says.

Normally, a properly purged, filled, and refrigerated Crowler or growler of beer should hold steady for several days, maybe up to a week, though

hop-forward beers should be consumed sooner. Don't delay. Crowlers and growlers are not museum pieces for your fridge, to be admired alongside leftovers and milk. There's no better minute for drinking a beer than this one.

WHOLESALE CHANGE: THE NEW WORLD OF BEER DISTRIBUTION

The seismic shifts in how and where we purchase beer have also shaken up beer distribution. In a less cluttered craft era, growing breweries signed with distributors and sent truckloads of stock hither and

Boston-area brewery Night Shift runs a distribution business that includes brands such as Chicago's Pipeworks.

yon, the arrival of, say, Stone heralded like manna from heaven. Praise be! Rain on the IPA desert! It was Manifest Destiny in the beer aisle, a tactic that's as outdated as a payphone.

America is marching toward ten thousand breweries, a glut of IPAs, lagers, and, well, IPAs. Curious consumers seek spanking-new releases. There's a premium placed on fresh and local and not the same-old brands on store shelves. To survive and thrive in this new paradigm, breweries are disrupting distribution

Robby Roda is the founder of Day One Distribution in Portland, Oregon.

and taking control of the delivery truck. Numerous breweries now operate full-fledged distribution divisions, including Colorado's Trve, Virginia's the Veil, and Massachusetts' Night Shift Brewing, which has self-distributed since its inception in 2012. "It kept growing and growing until we were like, 'This is turning into its own little business,'" says cofounder Rob Burns. In time, the brewery formed Night Shift Distributing and rented a former dairy-product warehouse. A fleet of refrigerated trucks delivers Night Shift cans and beer from breweries including New Jersey's Magnify, Chicago's Pipeworks, and Maine's Mast Landing. "We're placing an importance on the care and freshness of the product," Burns says. The

★ ★ ★

Advice: "Most consumers never realize or understand what it takes to get a beer on tap or into a store. How can small brands break through the noise if wholesalers continue to optimize for mega brewers? How does the industry continue to innovate if wholesalers aren't willing to take the chance on unproven new products? Combine all that with fewer wholesalers from consolidation, and we need beer lovers to pay attention to how beer gets on the shelf and maybe, just maybe, help find a better solution."

—Rob Burns, cofounder, Night Shift Brewing

★ ★ ★

Night Shift Distributing is based in a refrigerated warehouse formerly used for dairy products.

wholesaler piggybacks on Night Shift's 1,500-plus accounts, including Whole Foods, Trader Joe's, and Target, and offers an escape clause from the arrangement. "If you want to leave, we'll do it amicably and part ways," Burns says.

For Robby Roda, the founder of Day One Distribution, a fast dissolution was a big part of his business plan. He previously worked as sales director for Oregon's Cascade Brewing, dealing with distant distributors with varying degrees of giving a damn. "They were so reluctant to work with us and make changes to support us because they didn't have to," he says. Like most breweries, Cascade signed franchise agreements with its wholesalers, the middleman in America's three-tier beer distribution system. (The shorthand: breweries sell to distributors, which supply bars and stores.) The contract is a bit like a shotgun marriage. "It's almost like being held hostage by the Mafia," he says. "It's a big manipulation of the system."

Roda located a loophole. Oregon lets out-of-state breweries enter the market twice yearly for thirty days. The price of entry? Ten dollars per visit. "I so generously pay it each time," says Roda, who launched Day One Distribution in 2016. He brings in buzzing brands such as HenHouse Brewing and Phantom

Carriage for an instant. "It's basically on [tap] and gone," he says. Stock disappears before a brand's new-car smell wears off. "We keep it limited, keep it small, keep it special," Roda says.

Forward-thinking breweries are also creating special experiences by running mobile can sales far from home. "It's a cool evolution of how to sell beer," says Basil Lee, the cofounder of Queens brewery Finback. It has done pop-up sales in cities as far away as Miami, giving the Finback team a chance to be face-to-face with fans, an intimate retail experience not unlike buying a T-shirt from a touring band.

Depending on state laws, breweries either sell cans to a retailer or distributor or handle transactions

Bissell Brothers, in Portland, Maine, specializes in hazy and fragrant IPAs.

themselves. The latter isn't bad business; it's a boon for Hoptron Brewtique, in Patchogue, Long Island. "You get your cans and you can drink your craft beer," says co-owner Amanda Danielsen. Hoptron has hosted sales for New York City breweries including Interboro and Mikkeller NYC, the draft sales complementing a brewery's retail component. The events elicited a rare response: appreciation. "People kept saying, 'Thank you so much for having this.' In retail, it's not too common that someone says thank you for selling them a product."

GET FRESH: WHY FRESHNESS DOES AND DOESN'T MATTER

Brewers have done a terrific job of instructing drinkers to snappily consume beer. In particular, hazy IPAs' arresting fragrances and flavors are equally enticing and fleeting, a fiery relationship predestined to flame

★ ★ ★

Advice: Breweries most commonly stamp packaged-on dates on bottles' labels and necks, as well as cans' bottoms. Cans' blank silver canvas has become a bulletin board for breweries to post clever missives, memes, inside jokes, and more. I always look for a message before sending a can to its recycled fate. Also: I believe all breweries should code-date their beers. Ask why if they don't.

★ ★ ★

out. In America though, we like to take things to extremes. This may manifest itself as a near-maniacal desire to buy and consume beers as close to the packaging date as possible.

I kind of get it. Past-their-prime beers have burned me more times than my cast-iron pan. These scars gave rise to a peculiar tick: examining beer bottles and cans for evidence of the day the liquid took up residence. But I've learned not to celebrate youth too enthusiastically. "Sometimes beers coming right from the brewery are a little green and the flavors stand apart," Craft Beer Cellar's Schalow says of modern unfiltered IPAs. "Some beers need a few days to settle within themselves."

It takes time to really be your best self, and beers are no different. I've bought four-packs of IPAs that initially tasted like grass clippings blitzed in a Vitamix. A few weeks later, the beers became piña coladas poolside in Puerto Rico. And I'm not the only one who has noticed this phenomenon. "Inherently, especially with high dry-hopping rates, it's kind of inevitable to have a bit of roughness right out of the gate," explains Noah Bissell, head brewer at Bissell Brothers. He and his brother Peter have turned their brewery in Portland, Maine—one of my most very favorite cities*—into a must-stop on the Northeast's IPA trail.

Noah and Peter have seen vast columns of humans line up for their hop-intensified ales such as Substance and Swish, a nothing-but-net winner of a wheat-smoothed double IPA. The cans are almost exclusively sold directly from the brewery, where commerce can double as a teachable moment. "One of the greatest things about the shift to primarily on-premise sales is the opportunity for communication and to talk to people about nuanced things," Noah says.

Chief among them is an IPA's flavorful evolution. "We're pretty much in consensus here that a beer is not going to be its best on day one, no matter what the beer is," he says. "Once the beer is canned, something needs to happen exclusively in the can for that melding to happen in a positive way."

TAKE YOUR TIME

Do you like your beers a week old? One month? "The next step of freshness obsession is understanding the arc of maturation," says Dan Suarez, the cofounder of the Suarez Family Brewery. Suarez and his wife, Taylor Cocalis, run one of the more charming breweries I've discovered during my beer travels. The brewery sits in New York State's verdant Hudson Valley and operates a sunny taproom home to happy green plants, a dog nicknamed Chicken, and plenty of pilsners and lagers, all unfiltered.

"For me, I think most unfiltered beer styles are more dynamic," Suarez says. "If you filter a lager, the day you put it in the bottle it's the best it's going to taste." My favorite Suarez beer is Palatine, a German-style

*My wife and I were married in Portland and partied down at Bubba's Sulky Lounge. The bar has two light-up disco dance floors. Go and get your mind blown.

Dan Suarez brewing at Suarez Family Brewery. He and his wife run a brewery in New York State's Hudson Valley.

pilsner that I'd happily drink all day, every day. (The more hop-highlighted Qualify pilsner is also crazy good.) The pilsner is packaged unfiltered in 16-ounce cans, a living thing evolving according to its own timeline. "The day we put it in a can it's got a little cloudiness to it, a little turbidity, and a little bit of yeast binding to the hop constituents," Suarez says. "It's still a smooth beer, but it gives the impression of being hoppier and has a little bite."

One week later, Palatine clears up and becomes smoother, while the aromatics start cleaning up several weeks after that. Every week brings a new drinking experience. "These lagers mature gracefully, up to a certain point," Suarez says, emphasizing that good maturation hinges on beer being kept cold. "I think these should be drunk within two or three months, but at one and a half or two months, they're gorgeous."

Following the fruity evolution of a bombastic hazy IPA can be fun, but there's something to be said for savoring a beer that speaks in whispers, not shouts. "With a beer style that's so subtle, like a pilsner or helles, it makes it more exciting and nuanced to drink," Suarez says.

SIX IPAS TO BUY TO UNDERSTAND THE STYLE'S EVOLUTION

★ ★ ★

Mitch Steele knows more about IPAs than most every human. The author of *IPA: Brewing Techniques, Recipes and the Evolution of India Pale Ale* is a former brewmaster at Stone Brewing, where he helped sate and stoke America's lust for hops, hops, hops. Now the brewmaster and cofounder of New Realm Brewing, in Atlanta, Georgia (New Realm also operates a second facility in Virginia Beach, Virginia, the short-lived home of Green Flash's East Coast outpost), Steele is continuing to steer New Realm's IPA into new boulevards of flavor with the tropical Hoptropolis and lushly citrusy Hoplandia.

"People ask for juicy," he says of shifting tastes. "I think what we're seeing is that people really like the flavor of hops and don't necessarily like the bitterness of hops. There are not a lot of people that come in and say, 'What's your most bitter beer?'" This is an about-face from a decade ago, when aggressive bitterness was lauded, not loathed. International bitterness units (a.k.a. IBUs, a measure of a beer's bitterness) regularly topped triple digits, and beers with names such as Tongue Buckler and Palate Wrecker became America's most sought-after liquid currency. "Craft beer aficionados wanted the really bitter beers. The more hops, the more of a shock it was, the better it was."

The IPA will never reach its final resting place, forever a plaything for brewers to deliver elevated flavor, new hop cultivars sprouting from the ground each year. "There's so much breeding going on that, in the short term, I think hops are going to drive the varieties of the new IPAs," Steele says. It's fun to sip the latest lavishly hopped latest model, but the present and future are built on a historical foundation.

"Craft brewing is not a really old industry, but people seem to have left a lot of it behind. I think that's a shame, because there are so many great beers that came out 10, 20 years ago that are still wonderful beers, and people are missing a great experience by avoiding them," Steele says. "It's important to keep the history of craft relevant." Here are six time-tested IPAs he recommends seeking out, the past today's present for your palate:

1. Anchor Liberty Ale

2. Sierra Nevada Celebration Ale: "To me, they're [including Anchor Liberty Ale] two of the pioneering IPAs of craft beer. That's a good place start."

3. Harpoon IPA: "It's been around since the early '90s. That's a beer that was crazy popular in the Northeast for a long time. It really set the groundwork for everything that came after out there."

4. Stone IPA: "I don't say that because I worked at Stone. I would've said that anyway. Stone IPA to me was a groundbreaking beer before I even got to Stone."

5. Bell's Two Hearted Ale

6. Dogfish Head 90 Minute IPA: "Those beers [including Bell's Two Hearted Ale] tell you where IPAs were in the early 2000s. They're still relevant and still good beers."

The flavor of Suarez Family Brewery's unfiltered Qualify Pils will evolve over the course of several months.

BREWED AWAKENING: "Back in the late '80s I was living in Los Angeles and liked to frequent a dive punk bar by the name of Al's Bar. I loved the place. It was hot, small, full of graffiti, and the site of my very first real beer experience. The bar had about four beers on tap at any given time and it was Anchor Steam that first surprised and inspired me. I thought, 'Wow, beer can taste like this?' An entirely new world opened up to me that day. Little did I know how far it would take me!"

—Greg Koch, cofounder, Stone Brewing

TRANSFORMERS: MORE THAN MEETS THE BEER

Most new-breed hazy IPAs are packaged unfiltered, yeast and hop particulates still lingering in a bottle or can. Given time, certain yeast strains will create biotransformations of hop compounds, a doctorate-level concept that I'll condense to this: when yeast and hop oils hang out, chemical reactions transpire and wholly new aroma and flavor compounds are created. It's magic on a microscopic level.

"It turns out that certain hops, under certain conditions, under certain yeasts, during different stages of fermentation, will give up aromatics that have never before been released," says Jim Koch, the founder of the Boston Beer Company, which makes Samuel Adams beer. "That's the essence of a New England IPA."

Volatile sulfur compounds provide peaches, mangoes, apricots, oranges, papayas, and more fruits with appealing fragrances, the very ones that define today's IPAs. "There are sulfur-based aromatics in hops that are bound up with a protein molecule, and under the right conditions there's an enzyme produced that will break that bond," Koch says. "It happened, and we were like, 'Shit, that's not supposed to happen. Let's keep doing that.'"

Samuel Adams made the discovery while brewing dozens of test batches for what became the stylistically named New England IPA. The unfiltered beer ties a delicate sweetness to great big poofs of pineapple and grapefruit, sulfur-based aromatics the both of them. "A properly done New England IPA is a product of one of the first major new brewing techniques discovered in 100 years," Koch says. The science is still not largely understood and researchers are investigating the alchemy, a mystery that you, too, can investigate.

Feel free to put on a lab coat—or perhaps just jeans and a T-shirt—and perform informal research. One of Bissell Brothers' year-round beers is Reciprocal, a double IPA that's dry-hopped twice with fruity Australian varieties including Ella and Vic Secret. "It really doesn't start showing in a way that's ideal for me till three weeks to a month in a package," Noah says. "It's not just [that] it's this one perfect day and it falls off a cliff either. It's an arc. It's still Reciprocal on day one; it's just a little more aggressive version. That floats a lot of people's boats as well."

★ ★ ★

Advice: "Relatively speaking, the bigger the beer it seems the peak is a little longer down the road from packaging day. I'd like to think that's a good thing in the sense that people shouldn't be expected to drink something the first day they buy it. There shouldn't be this overarching pressure, like, 'Whoa, it's only getting worse.' It's beer! There shouldn't be room for this hyper-perishability element. Any beer shouldn't have a one-week shelf life."

—Noah Bissell, head brewer and cofounder, Bissell Brothers

★ ★ ★

★ ★ ★

Fun Fact: The importer B. United is so committed to freshness that it ships draft beer from Europe in temperature-controlled metal tank containers. They maintain near-freezing temperatures until the vessels arrive at the importer's Connecticut facility, where the beers may undergo a second or third fermentation, or be dry-hopped, before being packaged in sanitized kegs or cans. The payoff is that beers like Germany's subtly smoky Aecht Schlenkerla Helles Lagerbier and Italy's extravagantly fragrant Birrificio Italiano Tipopils pilsner taste as vibrant as they do in Europe. Seek them out for a fresh take on classic beer.

★ ★ ★

Jim Koch is a founder of the Boston Beer Company, which makes Samuel Adams beer, and recently acquired Dogfish Head.

DRINKING DESTINATION

Franconia: Where the Roots of Lager Dig Deep into the Hillsides

Joe Stange, freelance journalist and author of
Good Beer Guide Belgium

★ ★ ★

When I found a German-language dictionary from 1808, the first thing I did was look up the word *kellerbier*.

The meaning was simple: kellerbier is beer from the *keller*—that is, from the cellar. But it's not what you think—in this case the word stands for a cultural institution brighter and more entertaining than your creepy basement.

Quick geography lesson: Franconia is a hilly swath of northern Bavaria—roughly south-central Germany, with an eastern tip that reaches out to touch Czechia. The northeastern third is Upper Franconia, whose largest city is Bamberg, famous for its smoked beers and baroque architecture.

While Bamberg itself is fairly well known, the rolling countryside around it is an undersung playground for beer lovers. Per capita, there are more breweries here than anywhere in the world. Ride a bike in any direction and the next random village of a few hundred people is likely to have its own family-run brewery—and the beer will almost certainly be tasty, flavorful, and cheap. There is a pretty good chance that it will be kellerbier.

Author Joe Stange pours a Franconian lager.

You might even be drinking it in the keller.

About that word: In Franconia, *keller* usually means *biergarten*—because that is the beautiful thing that sprouted naturally from the spot where the beer was freshest. These kellers are enduringly popular, and their long benches under the trees are ideal spots to drink some of the world's most flavorful lager—and to ponder how lager came to exist in the first place. The experience is addictive; those of us who make the pilgrimage often find ourselves returning again and again.

Consider the Kellerwald in Forchheim, south of Bamberg. Its name is accurate: it's a forest full of cellars. The tree-covered hill is riddled with twenty-three tunnels once used by breweries to mature beer and then serve it directly to the public. They could drink it right there, take some home, or (more likely) both. Today it's a forest full of beer gardens, but the tunnels are still there.

Visit the Kellerwald on a hot day and you can feel—directly on your skin—the beer's reason for existing. Step into the shade and the temperature drops instantly, palpably. Those chestnut leaves don't just block the sun like a cheap umbrella; they transpire moisture and lower the temperature of everything below. Ask nicely and the keller staff might let you into one of the tunnels—where the temperature drops again. It was in dark, cool passages like these that lager yeast evolved and matured in ways that pleased Bavarian brewers and drinkers. Later, that yeast took over the world.

These days the breweries have fancy refrigerators, but the kellers still thrive. They are a pastime, an attraction, a frequent outing. A good one is as relaxing as any spa. Picture rows of long tables, shady chestnuts, and sprawling playgrounds. Kids run freely while grownups sit and drink and talk; bringing the family here for the day is neither selfish nor uncouth. Old fellers rap their

Book a trip to Franconia and this could be your beer.

knuckles on your table to say hi and goodbye, even if you're a stranger. Grub ranges from fresh crusty pretzels to infinite variations on roast crackling pork via cold sausage salads—none of it expensive.

Likewise, the beer is cheap. In many places around the region, a half liter still costs the equivalent of about two dollars (even in Bamberg, it rarely costs more than three dollars). If you walk into a pub and simply order a beer, they won't need to ask which kind. Many of these village breweries only make one.

Yet there is wide variety from village to village. Some kellerbiers are lighter, some are darker. Some are sweeter, some drier, and some quite bitter. There may be a distinct earthy-mineral taste, or not. There may be a rustic whiff of buttery diacetyl, as in neighboring Czechia, or not.

The brewery might call it kellerbier, or lagerbier, or ungespundet, or something else. To define them would be to enforce dogma where there is none. The point is to stick your nose in that krug, take another gulp, and enjoy the miracle of free time.

All signs point to beer in Germany's brewery-rich Franconia region.

THE POUR MOVE

GLASSWARE AND THE NEW RULES OF SERVING BEER

You don't easily forget the bar where you were strangled while sipping 32 ounces of foamy lager served in a Styrofoam bucket. The Turkey's Nest was a relic of a less refined Brooklyn, a bar where you could shoot pool and the breeze while watching sports on fuzzy TVs. My friends and I liked the Nest because the beers were cheap and bountiful, and even the strangulation—a disagreement over pool that I tried, and failed, to mediate—didn't pump the brakes on patronage.

Our vats of industrial lager were so inexpensive we never questioned the choice of container, much less the infinite foam hiding the liquid deep beneath the bubbly surface. Funny the difference fifteen years can make. Today, I cringe at both the landfill contributions and my cluelessness about what constituted properly served beer.

Great beer may originate from a brewery, but bars and their bartenders are the crucial last-mile link between producer and consumer. The very best of breed are stewards of both beer and customer experience, embracing the pageantry of pouring the perfect pint—we imbibe with our eyes first—and emphasizing a set of bedrock fundamentals, many of which are worth repeating at home.

Best practices begin by stocking style-appropriate glassware, washed clean, rinsed hot, and filled with beer flowing through regularly cleaned draft lines. Foam is no longer a flaw from an improper pour; it's a careful constructed feature that, at times, is worth a five-minute wait. In with patience! Out with poorly poured beers served in dirty glassware and riddled with off flavors. If you're at a bar, send them back, just like you would at a restaurant when served a well-done steak after ordering it medium rare. Also, do you really want to drink at a bar touting 120 taps? What's more may be less, especially when you realize that not every beer may be fresh.

With beer, I know I've stuck my neck out and made poor choices in the past. Here's how to make the best pour decisions possible.

EMBRACE THE TOUCH OF GLASS

Let's start with the red Solo cup. It's among the country's most iconic receptacles for party-hearty occasions, from picnics to tailgates, beer pong, music festivals, and wherever keg beer flows like a carbonated river. The disposable container is so beloved in pop culture that country musician Toby Keith once released a song called "Red Solo Cup," singing these immortal lyrics: "Red Solo cup / I fill you up / Let's have a party."

I love a raucous rager as much as the next person with a pulse, but I don't adore a cup that, like me, will soon be trashed. "Can I use this?" I'll ask as I pull a glass from your kitchen cabinet, hoping you've had just enough beer to not worry about doing morning dishes.

Now, I'm not standing on a cardboard soapbox fashioned from postconsumer waste. I'm here to extol the very many virtues of glass. Brewers make a series

Greg Engert is the beverage director of Washington, DC's Neighborhood Restaurant Group.

of deliberate decisions to create beers that smell and taste as good as they look; it's a shame to hide beer, sort of like spending big bucks on a fancy haircut and putting on a creased cap. "The full sensory approach to drinking includes the visual," says Greg Engert, beverage director of Washington, DC's extensive and influential Neighborhood Restaurant Group.

If a televised quiz show granted me one call to ask someone for beer help, I'd call Engert. He skillfully orchestrates the beverage program of ChurchKey, the lodestar of DC's beer scene; the forward-thinking Bluejacket brewery; and the Sovereign, where beer from Belgian breweries, such as De Blaugies, De la Senne (see page 148 for the brewer's insider scoop on Belgium), and De Dolle, is served according to his specifications. "With the right glass and the right temperature of service, you can gain access to the full array of flavors," Engert says.

> **BREWED AWAKENING:** "Hedwig Neven, brewmaster at Duvel, gave me a single word in 2004 I've used ever since. He was talking about why so many American beers meant to mimic those brewed in Belgium did not. 'They must be digestible,' he said. Digestibility. Drinkability. There's a difference, and you know it when you taste it."
>
> —Stan Hieronymus, author, *Brew like a Monk* and *Brewing Local: American-Grown Beer*

Fun Fact: Robert Hulseman, who invented the Solo cup in the mid-'70s, helped design the iconic Solo Traveler lid. You know it best from your cup of Starbucks coffee.

Shake It Off—A Farewell to Shaker Pints

Chances are the shaker pint won't deliver a full spectrum of flavor. It's the sturdily omnipresent straight-walled vessel that, like a codependent relationship, people can't quite quit. "The cheap durability and ubiquitous availability made it the go-to glass for bars, restaurants, and home drinking," Engert says.

Checking the cleanliness of a TeKu beer glass.

Stephen Hale is the ambassador brewer for Schlafly Beer, in St. Louis.

The shaker pint was once twinned to a mixing tin and used to—you got this one—shake cocktails. Like the Solo cup, shaker pints are prized as practical liquid-delivery vehicles. "They're robust and utilitarian, and it ends right there," says Stephen Hale, the ambassador brewer for Schlafly Beer, of Saint Louis. Even one of the shaker pint's chief attributes, its stackability, is a negative. "That scratches them," Hale says, leaving a telltale scuffed ring. Another downside is that the glasses are prone to slippage. Ever been bumped in a crowded bar and had a shaker pint slide from your palm, gravity sending the glass to the floor? My beer-stained sneakers are forever a reminder of my clumsiness. "I don't even drink water out of a shaker pint at work," Hale says.

★ ★ ★

Advice: "Don't use frozen glassware for beer," says Schlafly's Hale. "Fifteen years ago I went to a restaurant with my wife and ordered a Schlafly Pale Ale. The server brought it over and I had to chip icicles off the glass. I asked the server, 'Can I please have a glass that isn't frozen?' I swear, she took the glass, put it in a pan of boiling water, held it with a potholder, and then filled it with beer."

★ ★ ★

Perhaps the best reason to say goodbye to the shaker pint is because of your nose. "The glass does not allow for much aromatic investigation," Engert says. The glassware isn't big enough to create a pint's proper head, and the lack of curvature and stem makes beer nearly impossible to swirl,* which spurs a beer's carbonation and distinct fragrances. "The shaker neither focuses beer aroma nor stabilizes foam. In fact, that thick, cheap glass tends to warm the beer too quickly and encourage the quick loss of effervescence." Not that it mattered. "The lack of nuance in the beers produced by macrobrewers meant that any vessel would do," Engert says.

*I will so mail you *something* if you send me video of yourself swirling a full shaker pint of beer and not spilling a drop. Disclaimer: I'm not paying your carpet-cleaning bill.

A selection of essential beer glassware.

Take Stock

It's true that not any vessel will do when drinking beer. Think about dining at restaurants: Tableware sets expectations. Ten times out of ten, I'd wager, filet mignon consumed on a paper plate will deliver less pleasure than the pricey cut plated on bone china. Personally, I enjoy drinking from Germany's aroma-concentrating Willi Becher glass, a nice match of aesthetics, aroma, and hand fit. Engert also suggests a ridged English nonic pint "that combines durability with tradition" or an imperial Guinness pint glass. "These types of glasses are narrower, have some curve, and better convey a larger volume of beer while still attending to flavor maximizing," he says.

★ ★ ★

Advice: "If space is an issue, a great wine glass can handle most beer drinking needs with aplomb," Greg Engert says. He favors the One, designed by master sommelier Andrea Robinson.

★ ★ ★

HEY, WASH IT: A BRIEF GUIDE TO CLEANING YOUR GLASSES

Telling you how to wash glasses feels weird, like a remedial lesson in brushing your teeth. But we all fall into bad habits that can be hard to break. (I didn't mean to forget you, floss.) Here, Greg Engert dishes on proper cleaning protocol.

★ ★ ★

Show of hands. "For nicer, more delicate glassware, hand washing (rinse, rinse, rinse with hot water) is suggested," he says. "This keeps any logoed glassware from losing their labels via chipping and peeling."

Mostly say nope to soap. Engert recommends using a tiny dollop of soap. If you opt for a dishwasher, use a delicate cycle, keep glasses well spaced, and skip the heated drying. "If you can, open the dishwasher and let the steam escape," he says. Glassware should be air-dried or gently hand-dried, then polished as needed with a lint-free towel. He likes linen.

Mind the store. Glassware, like you and me, is affected by where it lives. Freshly painted, varnished, and lacquered cabinets, as well as plain wooden cabinets, can impart unwanted smells. (Word of caution: if you're stowing glassware between uses, cardboard boxes can also contribute aromas.) Also, you'll want to rest glasses on their bases. "Storing lip down likely does keep the inside a bit cleaner, but if you use and wash your glasses regularly, dust won't really accumulate," Engert says. Another plus: the rims will not chip or get dirty because of contact with the shelf or shelf liners.

Practice the smell test. "When it's time to use the glass, give it a sniff to see if any unwanted odors require more hot water rinsing, followed by proper drying," he says. "Presuming the glass has been cleaned and dried properly, a new cleaning or rinse will not be necessary. Also, give the glass a look to see if it could use a quick polishing refresher."

It's important to rinse a glass prior to pouring a beer.

This is not a bullhorn command to spend a paycheck on shiny new glassware. "You don't need 20 glasses," Hale says, a statement that's true for bars and homes alike. A do-it-all collection might include a wine glass; a tall, slender pilsner glass; a Willi Becher or nonic pint; a tulip, or a TeKu; and a full-bodied goblet or snifter.

Don't fret if you only own mason jars and mismatched Mickey Mouse glasses bought at the local thrift shop. "I would rather have somebody drink beer in a plastic cup or shaker pint if that's all they have," Hale says. "It's not a make or break. Don't stop drinking beer because it's all you have. Use whatever vessel you need to, but when you can find the appropriate glass it does make a difference."

STEP UP TO THE BAR

At bars, I was once afflicted by a peculiar kind of paranoia. *They are totally cheating me*, I'd think, scrutinizing a pint finished with a priest's collar of foam. *That should be beer.* I'd stew and stew, ignoring the real reason to be foaming mad: the hundreds of bubbles clinging to the walls of the glass, a telltale giveaway of dirty glassware.

Come and bend your elbows at the bar. A cold beer is waiting.

I'd spent so much time learning about styles and trying to decode the differences between, say, a kölsch and a cream ale* that I developed a blind spot for pouring and presentation. They can play a critical role in appreciating a beer, both aesthetically (got to get that Instagram!) and to your palate, that ultimate arbiter of taste. "I've always said that serving craft beer does not a craft beer bar make, since the daily cost, passion, and effort that go into properly serving that craft beer are far more demanding than procurement," Engert says.

In the mid-2000s, if I stumbled into a bar that served Sierra Nevada Pale Ale or Dogfish Head 60 Minute IPA, I'd dance a little jig. Compelling, fuller-flavored beer had just started soaking into the mainstream soil, a slow drip, drip, drip to tap lists at suburban chain restaurants and airports alike. The presence of beers from early-wave purveyors such as Great Lakes, Anchor, Deschutes, and Harpoon was a disco ball–lit advertisement that bars gave a damn.

Now you can drink great beer while attending a baseball game, flying through the clouds, or buying groceries *and* beer at stores like Whole Foods, Giant Eagle, and Lowes Food, where I found myself shopping during a South Carolina beach vacation several years back. Certainly, I took immense pleasure in grabbing hot dogs and other grillables while sipping 16 ounces of citrusy SweetWater IPA, clad in swim trunks, flip-flops, and a lobster shirt. However, it wasn't the beer that was novel so much as the deed, a tiny mutiny against standard social constructs.

It's why I dig drinking a tingly Berliner weisse or maybe a cloudy IPA on trains (#trainbeer) and other modes of mass transportation. The act, if but for a few train stops, returns beer to its rule-breaking roots. That's my response to a beverage that's gone from counterculture to mainstream commodity, availability metastasizing into excess.

*Kölsch is a German ale fermented at colder, lager-worthy temperatures. A cream ale, which contains no dairy products, is an indigenous American ale that's also fermented cold.

BREWED AWAKENING: "I've always tried to incorporate the things I love most into my life, with enjoying the great outdoors topping the list. Around college, it became clear that everything I loved shared one common thread: beer. Not just any beer, but great beer. Enjoying a quality beer during or after a day on the water, trails, or slopes made the day complete. Then it occurred to me that beer was my conduit to do the things I love while bringing my own twist to the party. I loved the entirety of the beer business and the artistry of designing a unique beer. I realized that marketing your product can also showcase your core beliefs and support causes dear to you. That's when I knew I had to open a craft brewery."

—Freddy Bensch, cofounder, SweetWater Brewing

THREE SIGNS THAT A BEER BAR CARES

★ ★ ★

Hint: it's not just about offering the latest double IPA.

Current affairs. "Look for updated websites, Untappd pages, and social-media feeds, including not just current beer menus and events but consistent engagement with guests. All of this shows daily effort and care," says Neighborhood Restaurant Group beverage director Greg Engert.

Everything in order. Once you're seated, look for the menu. Information should be up to date, and the menus or signage should be clean and orderly. Says Engert, "It should all look fresh."

Glass act. Check out the glassware selection and see if the bar stocks several different styles, the glasses visually free of soap and water marks. Additionally, look for clean tap handles and faucets and a well-organized setup behind the bar. "If any of the above is not happening, the line cleaning is likely being overlooked and the staff may not be getting the training they and the guests deserve," explains Engert.

From service to setting and selection, As Is, in Manhattan, is one of the city's best beer bars.

Wolf's Ridge Brewing, in Columbus, Ohio, works closely with kitchen staff on many beers.

Drafting a Solution

In recent years, bar draft lines dedicated to flavorful beer have multiplied faster than a calculator. Bars offering a couple of lines of golden ales, stouts, or IPAs—alternatives to all that lager—soon snowballed into bars offering fifty, sixty, one hundred, or, in the case of North Carolina's Raleigh Beer Garden, upwards of *four hundred* beers on tap. In an America obsessed with *more* (might I interest you in a Hardee's Monster Thickburger?), the supersizing of tap offerings is no surprise. As with bottle shops and stores, abundance is not always a good thing.

Master Cicerone Neil Witte agrees. "If a bar has 120 taps that says to me that they're being kind of lazy about selection," says Witte, the owner of industry consultancy Craft Quality Solutions and a contributor to the Brewers Association's definitive *Draught Beer Quality Manual*. "I know that sounds funny, but if you have 100 taps you don't have to put any thought into it. If a beer is available on draft, you're going to buy it. Also, you're probably not going through a lot of kegs very quickly and there's a lot of beer that's getting old."

Of course, some bars thrive on velocity. Denver's Falling Rock Tap House runs through its seventy-five-plus taps at a dizzying clip, especially when the bar becomes a brewers' clubhouse during the Great American Beer Festival. Houston's Hay Market offers seventy-five taps, including sour ales from Switzerland and Texas-brewed hefeweizens, plus a rarity—five cask ales. At Chicago's Hopleaf, the sixty-eight taps change so rapidly that the bar prints new menus up to six times a week.

Largely, though, fewer taps are the way to go. "If I were going to open a bar, I'd probably put 12 taps on," Witte says, adding that twenty taps would be his max. "You can get a good mix of styles and alcohol content and a diverse-enough selection for just about anybody that comes in."

BREWED AWAKENING: "As I set off on the earliest leg of my beer-drinking journey, I was lucky enough to have venerable Chicago tavern The Hopleaf as my navigator. The first time I sat on one of its barstools, I ordered a Kwak—likely because it was listed at the top of the Belgian-centric beer menu. What arrived before me was an ostentatious, wooden-handled, glass-holding contraption that I had no idea how to pick up, let alone drink from. The experience taught me three lessons that would serve me well for the rest of my beer career: a good bartender is invaluable; a great bar even more so; but the joy of new discovery is the best guide of all."

—Kate Bernot, beer writer and editor

JEFF "BRUNO" BRUNING

Partner, El Bait Shop

★ ★ ★

Beer drinking tends to be the least challenging part of the average person's day. Except if you're fishing for rounds at El Bait Shop.

"I always joke that it's ten times harder to drink all our beer than it is to run a marathon," says partner Jeff "Bruno" Bruning. "We just kept pushing the envelope and pushing the envelope, and the next thing you know we have 262 handles. That's just ridiculous. Anyone that would want to do that is insane."

Insane is a solid word to describe the Des Moines, Iowa, bar—and that's just the décor. One wall is a pictorial homage to pro wrestlers like Andre the Giant and Ric "Nature Boy" Flair near a *Where the Wild Things Are* mural. Did I mention there's also a working shower? You might miss that while staring, slack-jawed, at the stacked rows of shiny taps stretching into an IPA-filled infinity. Go on, snap a pic.

"I've argued that it's probably the second-most-photographed item in Des Moines, behind the state capitol building," Bruning says. "You can tell when somebody is a new customer. They're like, 'Holy crap, look at all those handles. Those aren't real, are they?'"

Jeff "Bruno" Bruning is one of the founders of El Bait Shop, in Des Moines, Iowa.

El Bait Shop's eclectic décor includes a *Where the Wild Things Are* mural.

They are real, and they're filled with really, really good beer, and lots of it. Homegrown Iowa breweries such as Barn Town and Toppling Goliath are sold alongside scarce kegs from Evil Twin and Grimm Artisanal Ales, and loads of rare Belgians. The tap list is a fast-moving turnstile, as more than fifty fresh beers rotate in weekly, a couple thousand new ones annually, creating a constant state of anxiety and expectation. "That's kind of our calling card," Bruning says. "It's always what you just missed, or you don't want to miss it."

El Bait Shop opened in 2006, born in Iowa with a blend of lunacy, optimism, and laser focus on craft breweries, or at least the local ones. On opening day, *three* breweries accounted for 52 of the 105 available lines. "We had 27 beers from Rogue," Bruning says of the Oregon brewery. It'd be tip-top to report that El Bait was met

with open stomachs and wallets, but trends slowly percolate to the country's core. One day, a partner sat down with Bruning and broke bleak news. Maybe 105 taps were too many. Maybe 80 were better. Maybe, just maybe, they should shut down and retool. "We were a little bit ahead of the game with craft beer in Iowa," Bruning says.

El Bait, which is the hoppy jewel of a hospitality group that counts a dozen-plus beer-focused concepts, survived the bumpy beginning and now faces a different suite of difficulties: how to store and serve all that beer. For years, Bruning tried packing El Bait with more and more beer, even filling a small metal box—seven feet by seven feet by eight feet tall—with twelve shelves of bottles and cans and fifty kegs. "Anywhere we could fit a handle, we were putting it in there," he says. "Then I was like, 'What am I doing?'"

(continued on next page)

Keeping tabs on 262 beers is a team effort including an Excel spreadsheet and a "beer traffic controller" who decides what goes on, and when, printing new menus as needed. "There's a lot of hands-on with our beer," Bruning says. "It's not that fun to do. If I didn't have people I 100 percent counted on and trusted and a management team working with me, we wouldn't be able to do this."

Curating the list requires constant vigilance, staying atop trends (hazy IPAs! dessert-like stouts!) and altering course as national brands lose luster. When Boston's Harpoon arrived in 2018, the brewery made tiny ripples in the drinking pond. "But if that would've happened five or six years ago, it would've been the biggest thing ever," Bruning says, emphasizing the ascension of drinking local. "When people come to town, they certainly don't have 515 or Toppling Goliath at their bar, so they want to try it."

The vast selection also makes it hard to highlight a single beer. During one event, El Bait poured the hankered-after beers of Scratch Brewing, which uses foraged ingredients like mushrooms and tree bark. Several months later, a beer that should've lasted a weekend remained. "With 262 taps it's impossible to hand-sell everything," he says. "You might know it's good, but not everyone knows it."

Customers often tell Bruning he should open another El Bait Shop here or there, a whole family of bars offering 262 beers on draft. Think ten marathons are tough? Try one hundred! No thanks. He sees the future, a future where 30 taps, or even 20 or fewer, makes the most sense. "Then you've got the velocity," he says. Still, El Bait thrives on abundance. Its 262 taps fill, then empty, then fill again, an outlier in Iowa and anywhere else. "Nobody in their right mind would do what we're doing," he says. "I feel like we're kind of a white buffalo."

Customers contemplate the wall of taps at El Bait Shop.

Keeping draft lines clean is essential to serving fresh beer.

The Dirty Truth behind Draft Beer

Witte has seen bars at their worst. He spent a combined nineteen years as a field-quality specialist for Boulevard Brewing and Duvel Moortgat USA, which bought the Kansas City, Missouri, brewery in 2013. Tap lines teeming with bacterial colonies, moldy equipment, walk-in coolers filthier than a flood-damaged home—name any sanitation nightmare, and chances are Witte has witnessed it.

At Boulevard, he led quality-control efforts by teaching distributors and retailers about the importance of properly installing, maintaining, and cleaning draft systems. These additional steps may seem unnecessary, like farmers visiting restaurants to ensure produce is stored in properly chilled refrigerators, the pots spotless. Many breweries extend the extra effort, and suck up the extra cost of education, for a simple reason: when a beer tastes bad at a bar, drinkers tend to point their pissed-off fingers at breweries.

"Most small brewers are going to be held responsible for any issues that pop up in the bar," Witte says. "If somebody had a bad Boulevard beer on tap, chances are they wouldn't give Boulevard the benefit of the doubt. They were going to assume that Boulevard brewed a bad beer."

Master Cicerone Neil Witte owns industry consultancy Craft Quality Solutions and contributed to the Brewers Association's *Draught Beer Quality Manual*.

We've all been disappointed by beer. That IPA you loved last week tastes less vibrant, psychedelics rendered in black and white. Or perhaps that porter has a vinegary twang. It must be the brewery's fault! Time to remove a star from its rating! Time to rethink

★ ★ ★

Advice: When a beer tastes a little off at a bar, ask the staff when the tap lines were last cleaned. "Draft lines should be cleaned every two weeks," says draft expert Neil Witte.

★ ★ ★

your outrage. Dirty tap lines can dull some of a beer's brighter, fresher aromas and flavors, as well as welcome bacterial infection, lending an unwelcome sourness.

This is not to absolve brewers of flawed beer and give them a fall guy or cover story. I've tasted some truly awful beer poured on spic-and-span tap lines. Just remember, no good brewery wants you to drink bad beer. "I used to tell people at Boulevard all the time that we couldn't afford to screw up that first impression," Witte says.

★ ★ ★

Advice: If you want to take a picture of your beer and some stubborn bubbles are stuck to your glass, tap it on the bar a couple of times to loosen them. It won't clean your glass, but it'll create a finer photo op.

★ ★ ★

Better Off Head

Call me shallow, but I've always believed that looks really matter when meeting a beer for the first time. And I have a swipe-right type: cool, bubbly, and finished with a fine top hat of white foam.

Friends, this is worth applause, not anger. Foam is no grand conspiracy to swindle you out of precious beer. "It can enhance the perception of all that stuff you like about the beer," Witte says. Foam is your friend! It acts like a butterfly net, capturing all those

Properly pouring Pilsner Urquell is as important as the beer itself.

volatile aromatics before they flutter off, never to be sniffed again.

On average, you'll want to see a beer with a half inch to an inch of foam, while styles rich in wheat (it promotes head retention) may be headier—looking at you, witbier and hefeweizen. If a beer is really foamy, you're totally within your customer rights to ask the bartender for a top-off once the beer settles. Just ask nicely. A single "please" goes a long way.

If you're pouring beer at home, here's the best way to get the right amount of foam: rinse a clean glass with cold water to remove lingering dust or detergent, lightly cool the glass, and set up a Slip 'N Slide for beer—the water provides a lubricated ride.

HOW TO TAKE YOUR PILS

★ ★ ★

In the Czech Republic, Pilsner Urquell is tradi-tionally served on draft three different ways, each one featuring varying levels of smooth, dense,

Varying levels of foam impact the flavor of Pilsner Urquell.

and wet foam. The standard *hladinka* is nearly half foam, offering a fine mix of sweetness and bit-terness. *Šnyt* is largely foam save for four or five fingers of beer at the bottom, an easy-drinking sip when you want a beer but not a full one—ideal for last call. Lastly, the all-foam *mlíko* (milk) is tradi-tionally an after-dinner treat, a sweet end to an evening. Key to the pouring is a side-pour faucet, which, in contrast to the normal open-close tap, acts more like a dimmer switch, Pilsner Urquell national sales rep Bryan Panzica told Good Beer Hunting. "You can get various degrees of foam," he said. "If you open the faucet 15 degrees, you'll get straight foam, but if you open it 90 degrees, you get straight beer."

To start, I tilt the vessel forty-five degrees and, targeting the middle on the side of the glass, begin pouring. When the beer halfway fills the glass, I slowly straighten it and finish pouring the beer down the middle, aiming for a half inch to an inch of foam. If a beer is really bubbly, sometimes I'll let it settle for fifteen or twenty seconds before topping off the foam. Drink. Repeat. Drink. Repeat.

At Your Service

Not every bar will serve picture-perfect beer. That's a bummer and, frankly, bad business. "When you're served a quality pint, it's not only a mark of quality for the establishment, but it also shows a dedication to a quality experience for customers," says Chris McClellan, a senior ambassador for the Guinness Brewery. "It looks better and shows that you care."

I'd be hard-pressed to name another brewery that cares more about their beer's appearance and quality than Guinness. The legendary Irish brewery, born in Dublin in 1759, has perfected the ritualized ceremony of serving beer. Chances are you know the drill, because it's repeated everywhere Guinness is sold, every hour of the day. Order the stout and a bartender will fill a glass three-fourths full with deeply ruby-hued liquid, then set it aside for about two minutes. The dissolved nitrogen waterfalls down the walls of the glass, then the bubbles surge to the surface and settle. The stout is topped off to the brim and served to customers, a liquid play with a beginning, middle, and end.

"There's buildup and a level of happy anticipation," McClellan says. "The pageantry that comes with Guinness is worth the wait." That's because the foam creates a better, more compelling beer. The creamy collar has a bitterness that contrasts the stout's sweetness, a bittersweet encounter from first taste to final swallow. "Specifically with that beer, you want a good combination of foam and stout in every sip," McClellan says. "It gives you a really, really lovely experience."

One sunny fall afternoon in downtown Manhattan, I tried my hand at pouring a Guinness under McClellan's careful tutelage. I nailed the pour and settle, then messed up the top-off by not closing the faucet properly. Instead of a smooth dimple, the head

Chris McClellan is a senior ambassador for the Guinness Brewery.

THE NITRO EFFECT

★ ★ ★

Guinness is nitrogenated, meaning that it's gassed up with a mixture of carbon dioxide and nitrogen. The element creates smaller bubbles than CO_2, helping create a denser head and smoother mouthfeel. Numerous breweries are now experimenting with nitro beer, most notably Breckenridge and Left Hand. Pro tip: to create the proper cascading effect, pour these beers hard—like, open the can and dump it in like you did as a kid with a box of cereal, hunting for plastic treasure.

Properly pouring a Milk Stout Nitro from Left Hand Brewing.

had jagged lines, like the tracks of a car swerving out of control. I succeeded in the broad strokes, but total deliciousness lies in the details.

"If you were in a competition, I'd have to dock you for that," McClellan said, assessing my less-than-masterpiece. I felt momentary sadness, then elation. Maybe I wouldn't win a medal, but I certainly held a swell consolation prize in my hand.

★ ★ ★

Fun Fact: In 2018, Guinness opened the experimental Open Gate Brewery and Barrel in Baltimore, Maryland. Guinness's first US brewery since 1954 serves the expected (stout!) and unexpected, offering citrusy IPAs and witbiers fermented with Guinness yeast.

★ ★ ★

Talking Out Our Problems

Chances are if I were served a subpar pint of Guinness even ten years ago, I would've swallowed my complaint and the beer. I mean, I still had beer, right? Today, I'd likely have a civil discussion with the bartender, respectfully expressing my displeasure in what's supposed to supply pleasure. More than ever, it's incumbent on consumers to hold establishments accountable for draft beer quality.

"There's only so far you can go with the major stakeholders like retailers, distributers, and brewers,"

Customers should talk to their bartender if they're dissatisfied with a beer.

Witte says. "You can get the word out, and they understand it, but there's only so much that they're going to do unless consumers start demanding it."

Say there's a corner sports bar that sells a little craft beer because it earns the owner a few bucks. Yeah, the glasses may contain more bubbles than a kindergartener's birthday party and the head may be reminiscent of depressed dish soap. But if the credit card receipts keep stacking up, there's no need to fix what's not broken.

"When you're talking to retailers, you have to talk in terms of money," Witte says. "You can't just say, 'Hey, you need to spend this much money to clean your draft lines because it's the right thing to do.' They'll be like, 'Whatever, nobody cares. I'm still selling the same amount of beer.' But if you can show them how cleaning tap lines will make them more money, they'll be more motivated to do it."

Your words and pocketbooks have the power to effect change, Witte says. Tell the staff that the beer tastes like I Can't Believe It's Not Butter!

KNOW WHEN TO SEND A BEER BACK

★ ★ ★

1. If a beer arrives in a stained glass or lacks a proper head, it should be sent back, advises Engert, beverage director of Washington, DC's Neighborhood Restaurant Group. In addition to glassware that's dirty or coated in detergent, beer can lose its foam because of improper pouring or because the glass sat too long before it was delivered. You wouldn't eat a restaurant's cold food, right? Treat beer the same way.

2. Return a beer if it smells of chlorine. "The bar has rinsed the glass with water high in chlorine, or has not thoroughly rinsed a glass sanitized with chlorinated sanitizer," Engert says.

3. "Don't let staff pour canned or bottled beer into a glass stained by lipstick, debris, or watermarks," Engert says. You should send that glass back and ask for a new one.

4. Anytime you feel that a beer is unacceptable or it's not as good as it could be, send it back. "People don't hesitate to send their food back when it's not right, but they often hesitate to send their beer back when it doesn't taste right," Witte says.

(That's the company's exclamation point, not mine.) Ask when the lines were last cleaned. Mention that you're going to start drinking beer down the block. "Once they start hearing that, again, that's the financial motive," Witte says. "That's what speaks to retailers."

⭐ ⭐ ⭐

Advice: A good bartender will never dunk a standard faucet in beer while filling your glass. The sticky residue creates an ideal bacterial hatchery.

⭐ ⭐ ⭐

HOW YOU STOMACH BEER

When I tell strangers I write about beer for a living, I generally get two kinds of responses. "Really? That's amazing," the first group will say, rhapsodizing about favorite beers and asking me mine. (My stock answer: The one in my hand. Zing!) The second set act as if they're forced to divulge a dark secret. "I don't like beer," they'll say. "That's OK," I'll say, becoming a kind of beverage therapist.

I try to explain that there's a beer for everyone, as many different flavors as there are ways to consume breakfast, lunch, and dinner around the world. They'll nod, a nod I know well. *You're saying words, but I*

Master Cicerone Max Bakker is the senior educator for Anheuser-Busch InBev.

don't believe them. I get it. It's damn near impossible to change somebody's mind with words alone, verbal battles fought to stalemates online every minute, every day. "Beer also makes me full."

This is where I can tap the internet to effect change. On YouTube, there's a Business Insider video titled "A 'Beer Sommelier' Explains How Pouring a Beer the Wrong Way Can Give You a Stomach Ache [*sic*]." It looks like clickbait designed to hold eyeballs for maybe two minutes. Watch it, and you may never drink a beer out of a bottle or can again.

In the video, Master Cicerone Max Bakker, the senior educator for Anheuser-Busch InBev, pours a beer into a glass carefully, barely creating any foam. Then he dunks a rolled-up napkin into the beer, causing it to foam like a nine-year-old's volcano science experiment. "That's 100 percent what's going on in my stomach if the beer isn't poured properly," he says. "Now you think, 'Wow, every time I had beer I get really bloated.' That's what's going on." He pours another beer, this one with plenty of head ("Foam always turns into beer," he explains) and goes in for another dunk. The bubbles are about as excited as I am while cleaning my toilet. "It's not agitating my stomach because I had broken that CO_2 out in the glass," he says.

The video has been viewed more than one million times and includes no shortage of, umm, enlightened comments. "This takes away one of the best parts of drinking: massive beer burps." "I don't wanna wait precious minutes for my six-inch-head to dissipate." "I prefer to shotgun my beers." "I like turtles."

"My brother and I like to read the comments when we're drinking beer," Bakker tells me one afternoon over beers at Arts and Craft Beer Parlor, in New York City's Greenwich Village. We're here because the bar's squeaky-clean tap lines pump out super-fresh beer with the proper amount of fizz. To wit: our matching pints of Greenport Harbor Black Duck Porter. It's dry and roasty, whispering coffee, cocoa, and . . . what's that flavor? Butterscotch? Should it be there?

"Low levels of diacetyl are totally acceptable in an English-style porter," Bakker says of the fermentation by-product. If I were posted at a dingy dive, I might've pondered returning the beer. But with immaculate tap lines, there's no mistaking the brewer's intent. We finish our first pints and order another round of the same porter, initial weirdness turning into a craving. "It's the two-beer test," Bakker says. "Truly great beers pass the test."

★ ★ ★

Advice: To preserve maximum flavor (aroma, taste, mouthfeel), the best brewers code-date packages, ship their beer cold, and sell it fresh. "Beer isn't perishable, flavors are perishable," says Master Cicerone Max Bakker. Exposing unfiltered or bottle-conditioned beer to extremely warm temperatures could lead to yeast autolysis, in which the organisms die and burst open, releasing their fatty lipids, acids, and sulfurs into the liquid. The odorous result: a meaty aroma reminiscent of burned rubber.

★ ★ ★

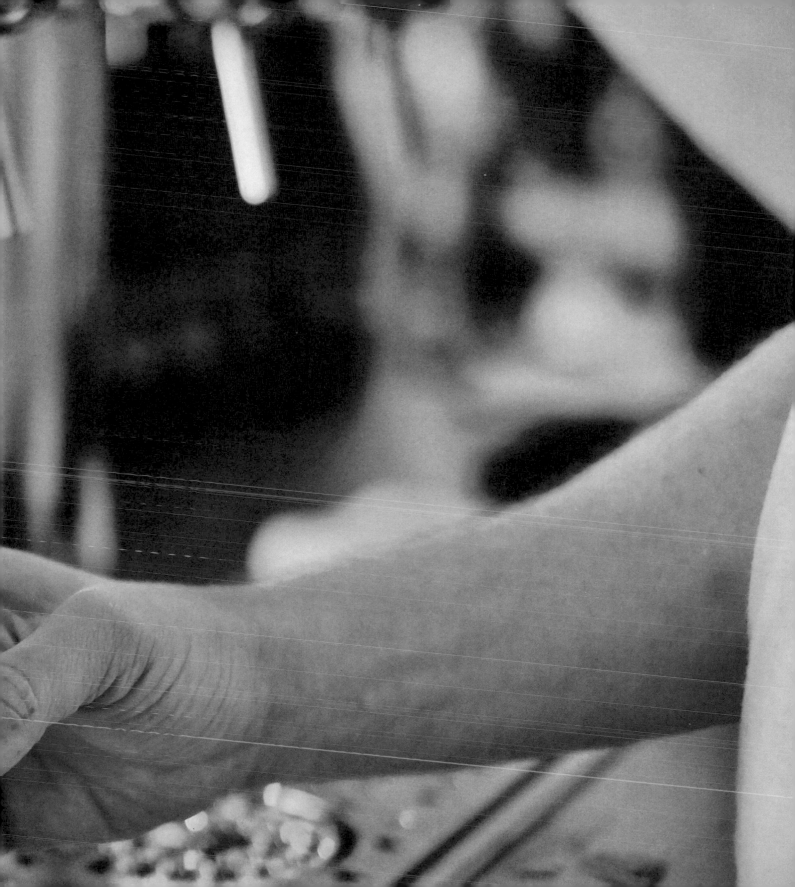

BE STILL, MY BEER

Most breweries work hard to ensure that their beers are properly effervescent: not too fizzy, not too flat, the bubbles just right—Goldilocks and the Three Beers, a story as old as 2019. Here's the plot twist: some breweries are saying goodbye to bubbles and releasing beers as still as week-old seltzer.

"The expectation of beer being carbonated is pretty deeply ingrained," says Paul Arney, the founding brewer of Ale Apothecary, in Bend, Oregon. It doesn't have to be that way. Uncarbonated beer is commonplace in Belgium, where spontaneously fermented lambics are packaged still in kegs or plastic bags. The benefit is that when you eliminate carbonic acid (CO_2 dissolved in an aqueous solution), sour beers aren't as sharply acidic and can be easier to consume.

"You can have sparkling wine and you can have still wine, and it's kind of dependent on the character of the wine," Arney says. He uses wood, wild yeast, and souring microbes to create distinctive small-batch beers such as the tart, earthy, and tropical Sahalie and Sahati, produced in a lauter tun (it separates wort from grains) carved from a tree and lined with spruce branches. "I let my inner brewer lead me," Arney says.

Annually, Arney makes a dark sour ale called Be Still. It's flavored with cascara and cocoa nibs and aged in pinot noir and rye whiskey barrels. "If you add carbonic acid, that's going to be a one-dimensional, really sharp beer," Arney says. "The thought was,

Like bagged wine, Colorado's Primitive Brewing packages its spontaneously fermented beers uncarbonated in boxes.

when we pull the beer out of the barrel and present it still, it's going to allow that roast to become part of the beer and not mask the cocoa nibs and cascara."

Other breweries on the no-bubble bandwagon include Side Project Brewing, which has produced still beers such as the Belgian-style Trail Dubbel, aged in red-wine barrels, and the Texas farmhouse brewery Jester King. Each year, it releases a still version of its SPON series of spontaneously fermented beers, using customer education to help alter ingrained beliefs. "It comes down to these lingering opinions that beer is this cold, fizzy beverage," says founder and owner Jeffrey Stuffings. "There's this expectation that it will be this effervescent, force-carbonated thing."

Perhaps the most antibubble brewery is Primitive Brewing, in Longmont, Colorado. The brewery sells its spontaneously fermented, barrel-seasoned sours in boxes, just like bagged wine. "We're trying to use the box as a way to set the expectations. Most people in America are used to boxed wine and the idea that, OK, if I'm going to pour wine from a box, it's not going to be Champagne," explains cofounder Brandon Boldt. "This is going to be a still, cellar-temperature beverage that can be consumed en masse."

Boldt knows still beer won't be everyone's cup of beer. What it can do is showcase the flavors that beer can take on when you take carbonation out of the equation. "It won't be for everyone, but it can help you understand what you actually like and what profiles taste best to you," Boldt says. "Some people

have told me, I expected to really dislike still beer, but I'm loving it. We've also had people come in and say, 'Nope, not for me.' That's exactly what you want to hear when you're trying something different from the mainstream and trying to push people's perceptions of what beer should or can be."

★ ★ ★

Fun Fact: Paging Mister Softee: one cool trend to watch is breweries using soft-serve and slushie machines to dispense beer, an experiment in both flavor and texture. Of note, Sweden's Omnipollo, the United Kingdom's Buxton, and Maryland's Burley Oak are helping popularize the practice.

★ ★ ★

THE BEST BEERS COME TO THOSE WHO WAIT: MEET THE SLOW-POURED PILSNER

I assumed there were certain truths to the world. The sun rises. The sun sets. And there is only one way to pour a pilsner—pretty fast. But while visiting Denver's Bierstadt Lagerhaus, which specializes in German-style lagers, I found myself waiting around five minutes for a glass of ghostly pale pilsner, the head as dense as whipped egg whites. This was the brewery's Slow Pour Pils, a revelation that, like a foam-crazed prophet, I wanted to reveal to everyone. "You may be waiting longer for it to arrive, but the satisfaction you get is a bit of a rush," Victory Brewing cofounder and brewmaster Bill Covaleski says of slowly poured pilsners, which the brewery has offered since it opened in 1996. "You don't rush through it because you feel compelled to, you rush through it because each sip is exciting."

In Germany, pilsners are traditionally poured slowly, with intention, a process that goes a little like this: Bartenders aggressively pour a beer into the center of a glass, filling it with a two-to-one ratio of foam to beer. The beer sits by its lonesome for a few minutes, letting the foam settle, and then more beer is poured. More foam. More waiting. At last, the beer is topped off and served, a process that can take up to five minutes. (You can follow those same steps at home.)

"When you're handed a slow-pour pils, it looks dramatically different," Covaleski says. "The head has risen higher and is fluffier. Someone who doesn't understand why all those conditions exist will say, 'Wow, that looks delicious.'"

It tastes better, too. The pouring technique expresses carbon dioxide, softening carbonation and bitterness while concentrating aromatics in that

The Slow Pour Pils at Bierstadt Lagerhaus, in Denver.

BREWED AWAKENING: "I was on my way to the Czech Republic—my first time drinking in Central Europe—and I wasn't that excited. I was an ale drinker and I wanted American IPAs and barrel-aged stouts, not the boring lagers I'd rejected when I discovered more interesting beers. But with one gulp of fresh Czech pilsner, my drinking changed forever. It was so delicious and compelling and exciting and I drank it all night. That was the moment that my drinking jumped to the next level, the level where you look back and start to appreciate the traditional and timeless beers and don't just look toward new ones."

—Mark Dredge, author, *A Brief History of Lager: 500 Years of the World's Favourite Beer*

Victory Brewing cofounder and brewmaster Bill Covaleski demonstrates the slow-pour pilsner.

glorious head. "It's not bringing so much gas into your stomach," Covaleski says, underlining a delicious contradiction: you might wait longer for a slowly poured pilsner, but chances are you'll drink it faster than a normally poured pilsner.

"You can plow it down," Covaleski says. "I certainly don't want to come off as saying this is the shotgun version of draft beer, but physically, there are conditions set up that entice you to drink the beer faster." I'd like to see this trend quickly catch on in America, but it may take time to convince bars to take their time. "It doesn't happen in a void," Covaleski says. "No one comes up and says, 'Hey, are there different ways to serve that beer?'"

DRINKING DESTINATION

Prague: Where Pilsners Are Served at Playgrounds and State Dinners

Evan Rail, author of *Why Beer Matters*

★ ★ ★

The gorgeous capital of the country that consumes the most beer per person every single year, Prague is a dream destination for many beer lovers. That's not to say it's perfect in every way, of course. If you're interested in acquiring a chestful of new Untappd badges, be aware that you probably won't find a ton of variety in the Czech capital, at least not in terms of beer

Prague beer author and journalist Evan Rail.

styles. In the homeland of pilsner brewing, pilsner is 99 percent of what people drink.

Instead of lots of different kinds of beer, what you'll find is lots of beer, period, and one of the world's greatest *living* beer cultures—a place where beer is part of society at every level. Feel like catching some Dvořák or Smetana at the opera gala? Of course they serve Pilsner Urquell. Attending a state dinner at Prague Castle? You'll definitely drink some fine lagers. Taking your kids to their favorite neighborhood park? The kiosk next to the playground serves fresh draft beer, and no one will look at you funny if you hold your beer in one hand while you push your kid on the swings with the other.

In fact, beer is so pervasive in Prague that just a few days here can really alter your perspective. If you're a modern-day Ahab, constantly chasing whales back home, in Prague you'll start to understand the appeal of extremely low prices and widespread availability, two of the main reasons why Czechs drink almost twice as much beer as Americans. If draft beer is cheaper than bottled water (which it is here), why wouldn't you drink beer instead of water? When the beer in question is a high-quality Bohemian pilsner—redolent with spicy Saaz hops and rife with the rich malt of a traditional decoction mash—you shouldn't even have to ask.

And if you think that good beer is something to celebrate, in the Czech Republic you'll see that great beer can be enjoyed without any party required. Stop by a traditional Czech *hospoda*, such as U Pinkasů in central Prague, and you'll find the off hours filled with retirees sipping a slow one alone while perusing the sports pages, or salesmen ordering a *světlý ležák*, or pale lager, while they go over their spreadsheets. In Prague, beer is the drink of choice for just about everyone, from college girls to construction workers, on just about every occasion.

You'll discover even greater depths of beer culture the more time you spend here. Just like "three sheets to the wind" and other nautical expressions in English, expressions about *pivo* color the Czech language, such as "Kde se pivo vaří, tam se dobře daří" (Where beer is brewed, there, life is good). Hops, cultivated here for more than a thousand years, are not an obscure herb known only to connoisseurs,

but one of the country's most important agricultural products. The same goes for barley. Beer is such an important part of Czech culture that Prague even has a brewing high school, where students graduate with brewmaster degrees, fully prepared to go to work producing high-grade lagers at just eighteen years of age.

Prague is a super-fun travel destination. But it's also educational, teaching us that great beer can be both a refined luxury and an everyday occurrence. Order a half liter of Únětice's flagship pilsner at the beautiful brewery restaurant and you'll wonder how something that costs so little can be so richly aromatic and bittersweet. And who knows? After a second glass, you may just decide to stay here forever.

Old Town Square, Prague, a must-stop for a beer or two on any visit to the Czech Republic.

SCENTS AND SENSIBILITY

CRACKING THE CODE ON FLAVORS AND AROMAS

It's been a couple of decades since I told the story of the keg in the laundry room. It was the summer of 1996 and I'd just graduated from high school. College was dead ahead and my parents and younger brother and sister were on an eighteen-day trip. I'd opted to stay behind and hang with friends before we scattered in the collegiate winds, never again to be so close.

Which meant we needed beer.

We convinced a friend's older brother to buy us a half barrel of Icehouse, a lager that was one of America's first so-called ice beers. Before aging, Icehouse is cooled to twenty-seven degrees to create ice crystals that, according to so much marketing speak, lend a smoother taste. I remember less than zero about the beer's flavor. To us, it tasted like freedom, a magical reservoir of liquid that somehow lasted for the lion's share of eighteen days in the laundry

Getting to know a beer requires getting to understand its aroma, for brewers like Zack Kinney, a founder of Brooklyn's Kings County Brewers Collective.

dioxide pushing beer out at a steady pressure, oxygen banned from the party. Still we drank, ignoring the dwindling carbonation and what were increasingly off aromas. We didn't know any better. Maybe beer was supposed to smell and taste like that?

Uh, no, it shouldn't. Two decades later, I've learned to approach beer a little more critically, instead of treating it as simple happy juice spat from a spigot. This doesn't mean I analyze every beer as intensely as scholars do hieroglyphics, meticulously decoding the liquid's deep mysteries. Instead, I embrace a bit of mindfulness, taking a few seconds to ponder a pint before sending it to its destiny, my stomach.

In the beer industry, making sense of the sensory has become an increasingly important part of the business. The best breweries, I've learned, are the ones that create quality-control programs to ensure their beers are as unblemished as an actress's Oscars makeup. Beer judges have a slew of tricks (yes, you should sniff your arm) to help them accurately assess a beer, as well as track trends in unwanted flavors—there's a reason so many beers reek of baby diaper. Consistency, as unsexy as that word might seem, has become many breweries' most important mission, the difference between dependably great beer and something worth sipping once and never again.

Properly appraising a beer's flavor and aroma does not require arcane wizardry or some costly mechanical contraption. We're all born, more or less, with all the tools we need to decode what we're drinking. Let's start making sense of scents.

room, bobbing in a trash can of room-temperature water, the beer poured from a hand pump, then later into empty two-liter bottles of Diet Coke. How we treated that beer was a party foul on numerous levels.

Let's start with hand pumps, a convenient if aromatically ruinous method of dispensing beer. The devices introduce oxygen, ushering in oxidation and accelerating the loss of carbonation. They're great for tapping a keg you'll crush in one night, not eighteen of them, which is a task fit for a kegerator, carbon

MAYBE YOU'RE BORN WITH IT

Some people are blessed with a particularly fortuitous roll of the genetic dice. Michael Phelps is part fish. Serena Williams precisely thwacks tennis balls at warp speed. Steph Curry can toss basketballs through hoops better than most of the human race. But not everyone is blessed with physical prowess—notably, this five-foot-four failed Little Leaguer. But most of us are born with a nose, a tongue, and a brain, the core tools required to better understand beer.

"I believe anyone can learn how to taste beer, just like anyone can learn to draw or to play music," says *Beerology* author and Toronto resident Mirella Amato, who in 2012 was the first non-US resident to become a Master Cicerone. She's built a career out of educating people about beer, consulting for restaurants and retailers, and judging some of the globe's most prestigious beer competitions, including the World Beer Cup and Brussels Beer Challenge. So yeah, you can trust her tasting insight.

"I've spent more than ten years doing public tastings with groups of people and I can state, with confidence, that most if not all people have a much better palate than they think they do," she says. "They can pinpoint those flavors. The piece that's missing and needs to be developed is identifying that flavor, giving it a name, and sharing it. How many times have you tasted something and thought, I know what that is, but your brain is not making the connection. What is that flavor? That, to me, is the biggest piece of the training—being able to connect these thoughts."

Master Cicerone Mirella Amato is the author of *Beerology*.

Advice: "The only way to understand what you like and what you don't like is try a bunch of beer. I hate to break it [to you], but that's really it. You know what you like. Just because you think you don't know enough about beer, don't be ashamed to say, 'I really don't like this.' That's not a problem. People feel they're not getting it right when they say they don't like something. There's this nervous twitch that happens like, 'Is that OK?' Actually, it's totally OK. It's normal to have opinions. Don't be shy."

—Dr. Henry "Hoby" Wedler, cofounder, Senspoint Design

Word Up

Imagine if I wrote this book with just a few dozen words, a brief and blunt collection of nouns and verbs used to crudely convey emotion and action. Book: boring. We often draw from a linguistic well about as deep as a footbath to describe food, drink, and even that strange odor emanating from the fridge's dark, damp recesses.

"When it comes to sight, we have so many words to describe things," Amato says. "If I'm looking at an orange, for example, I can say that it's orange in color, it's got a waxy finish, it's mottled. I can describe its size, and whether it's pocked or not.

When it comes to the aroma, what do we say? It smells like an orange. There isn't even a word for that smell."

Stock your language arsenal by embracing a curious, roving palate. "Try as many foods, drinks, and experiences as you can. Even the stuff you know you won't like will open your eyes, making it easier to identify flavors and aromas in the future," says James Watt, the cofounder of BrewDog and a Master Cicerone. "Pay close attention to how things taste, smell, and feel in your mouth. You might want to scoff the rest of the chocolate cake in front of you, but try it with a swig of kriek and see what happens. Or next time you're enjoying a Thai chicken salad, throw a citrusy pale ale at your palate and find out if it works. Take notes. Experiment. Go wild."

This speaks to a broader certainty: it's impossible to identify a flavor that you've never tasted, like fumbling through a foreign language with hand gestures and wild pantomimes. "You can read in a book about how an off flavor like acetaldehyde smells and tastes like green apple, but it doesn't taste *exactly* like a green apple," Amato says. "If you haven't encountered it in the wild and really been able to identify it, you're not going to recognize it later just based on a description in a book."

"Acetaldehyde is interesting to me, because it can come across as latex paint or slightly plastic-y," says the Bruery founder and Master Cicerone Patrick Rue. "But I only recognize it when it's green apple or a bruised red apple."

BrewDog cofounders James Watt (left) and Martin Dickie.

That's why it's important to drink outside your comfort zone. It's easy to mock that mass-produced ice lager or an IPA flavored with toasted marshmallows, vanilla, and cherry blossoms. (It's called a Cherry Blossom Mochi IPA, and Decadent Ales makes it.) Ridiculing what's unusual, or what we don't understand, is a time-honored human practice.

Put preconceived notions on ice. Drinking different beers is the best way to break free from biases and have a broader understanding of beer flavor. "When I'm judging competitions, I will routinely go out of my way to request the light lager category or pumpkin beers—styles I'm less familiar with and don't

drink on a regular basis," Amato says. "It keeps your palate well rounded."

The Write Stuff

I can tell you that my crockpot of three-bean chili tastes spicy and complex, the layers of flavor delivered by coffee, cocoa, and cinnamon. What does that mean? That's just a word stew. You need to taste each element individually to associate a foodstuff with a flavor profile. Me, I learn best by writing things down, whether it's pen to paper, fingers to keyboard, or thumbs to smartphone. The act creates mental glue, permanently affixing information to my synapses and

Jules Lerdahl, Ninkasi Brewing's sensory specialist.

neurons. Jotting down impressions can help you construct a dictionary of descriptions, ready-access associations of flavor and fragrance.

When her tasting journey started, Amato used the exacting Beer Judge Certification Program style guidelines as a compass to guide bonds between words and real-world experience. "They describe, in extreme detail, what each different style of beer should taste like," she says. "I actively sought out classic examples and I would taste and read at the same time and try to make those connections. Then I moved to tasting and writing my own notes."

For at least three years, she documented every beer she drank, a level of commitment few may match. There's no number I can point to that'll unlock expertise, like a game show's grand prize. "Eight hundred and forty-seven beers! You're our new top taster!" What writing does is force you to pay attention. And as we all recall from school, when you pay attention, you can learn something new.

SOMETHING IS OFF: TRENDS IN FLAVORS

★ ★ ★

Beer trends are not just about the latest IPA variant. Flaws also tend to be faddish in nature. "As I'm judging competitions, I get to see the ebb and flow of off flavors. They're everywhere and then they disappear," says Master Cicerone Mirella Amato. "There are some spectacular off flavors out there." Here are four you might come across:

1. **Butyric Acid**
   "It's that vomit, blue cheese, distinctly unpleasant note," Amato says. It's become more prevalent with the rising popularity of quickly soured beers such as gose and Berliner weisse (see page 162). "You're trying to create conditions that are ideal for cultivating *Lactobacillus*. If you're not careful with the pH and the temperature, you're going to open the door to all kinds of other bacteria. One of those is *Clostridium butyricum*, which is going to give you that butyric acid."

2. **Isovaleric Acid**
   Did your beer come with an aromatic side of rotten Parmesan cheese or sweaty, stinky feet? You can thank this fatty acid found in old hops. A decade ago, many brewers were "trying to sneak in old hops at the bittering stage and cover it up with fresh hops at the flavor and aroma stage,"

Amato says, adding that she regularly noted the acid in IPAs.

3. **Tannins**
   "I've also become sensitive to tannins," she says. "It's like an over-steeped tea or a really drying sensation. It has to deal with how malts are being treated, because tannins are being extracted from the malt husks."

4. **Tetrahydropyridine**
   Commonly called THP, the compound's flavor is often compared to Cheerios or Cap'n Crunch and, at high levels, urine ("mousey" is a nice euphemism). *Brettanomyces* and lactic acid bacteria can both produce THP, making it common in mixed-culture beers that utilize both wild yeast and souring bacteria. THP is an ephemeral flavor, and given time it will vanish.

"Getting in the practice of writing can really help you focus your mind and pick out what's different about the aroma and the flavor," says Jules Lerdahl, Ninkasi Brewing's sensory specialist. "Instead of just sitting there and downing the beer in front of you, try to break it apart into categories and think about it as if you were going to formally evaluate it."

A Recommendation for a Brief Appraisal

A formal evaluation feels like a pretty clinical act, like visiting the doctor for a checkup or a having a mechanic get under your car's hood. Assessing a beer should be fun and informative. Think of it as a speed date featuring a series of five-pointed, revealing questions:

1. What does the beer look like?
2. How does it smell?
3. How does it taste?
4. What's the mouthfeel?
5. How does it finish?

These aren't big asks, but they can pay big dividends. "When you order each new beer, stop what you're doing and take a moment to really [consider] that first sip and think, Does this taste different than the previous beer I had?" Amato says. "Is it sweeter? Is it more bitter? Do I like it more? Do I like it less? Is there any flavor that sticks out?"

The process can be pretty brief. "You don't have to sit there for twenty minutes, but just upfront, assess how the beer has been served and what it looks like," says Ryan Daley, a Master Cicerone who has spent more than fifteen years in beer, working for retailers, breweries, and wholesalers alike, most recently as a senior beer educator for Anheuser-Busch InBev. "There's this notion of thinking while drinking. The good news is, you can do both. You can drink, or you can think while you drink."

Master Cicerone Ryan Daley.

If you pay attention to a beer, Daley says, it'll reveal itself in different ways, like a date warming up and showing a different side. "The first few things I perceive from my initial smell are going to be different than what I start to perceive halfway through," he says. "All of the sudden these little nuances start to come out. You're only going to appreciate those if you take your time and [are] thinking about it a little bit."

Beer is both big picture and tiny details. Consider a Wes Anderson film like *The Royal Tenenbaums* or *Rushmore*. Rich narrative arcs are complemented by a hyperfocus on framing, scenery, and costuming that heighten enjoyment and command close, repeated viewings. "I'll go out with friends who are not in the beer industry and we'll order the same thing and about halfway through the pint I'll say, 'Ah, the orange note in this beer is amazing,'" Amato says. "They'll go back and taste and be like, 'Oh yeah, there is an orange note. I didn't notice.' It's not that they didn't notice. The brain recorded it on some level. They just didn't think about it. You'll enjoy your beer a lot more if you know what it tastes like."

> **BREWED AWAKENING:** "Probably 15 years ago, my wife and I were visiting my in-laws in Baltimore. I went out in the afternoon to get a bite to eat and grabbed a pint of Tröegs Nugget Nectar that was so fresh, so aromatic, so flavorful. The glass, the beer's orange-amber color, the one-inch collar of foam, the hop aromatics, and the malt character were hitting on all cylinders. When everything comes together, that's what makes beer so unique. And it really starts with how the beer is poured and presented, not just the flavors."
>
> —Ryan Daley, Master Cicerone

* * *

Fun Fact: To demonstrate the difference between taste and flavor, the Cicerone Certification Program suggests this clever test: Plug your nose, pop a random jelly bean in your mouth, and chew. You'll only note sugar and texture. Unplug the appendage and exhale through your nose, and volatile aromatics will flood olfactory receptors and reveal the candy's full flavor snapshot.

* * *

DR. HENRY "HOBY" WEDLER

Cofounder, Senspoint Design

★ ★ ★

It's best to begin with a disposable plastic water bottle. If one's handy, pick it up, shut your eyes, and caress the carafe. The plastic will probably be pliant, ridged, and curved for ideal palm placement. With your other hand, unscrew the stiff cap and hydrate, cool wetness to lips, tongue, throat, and stomach. The package serves a sole function, unremarkable on its trek to the trash except for that rough bump at the bottle's base. Feel it?

"Many mass-extruded bottles have a little nub at the bottom that really annoys fingertips, especially if you're a person like I am who sticks a pinky under the bottle when I take a drink," says Dr. Henry "Hoby" Wedler. "One of the things to think about with bottle design is that you don't want any pokey parts. Simple, almost silly stuff like this makes our work shine."

The cofounder of Senspoint Design, in Petaluma, California, views the world differently from most. Dr. Wedler was born blind, and his disability is an extra-special ability to see what others may overlook. "We tend to focus so much of our energy on our vision," he says. "I've found studies that say 85 to 90 percent of the information we take in comes from sight. That means we have four additional, perfectly good senses for absorbing and understanding 10 to 15 percent of the world."

Dr. Henry "Hoby" Wedler, who is visually impaired, brings a tactile expertise to his designs.

At Senspoint, he works with restaurants, real estate interior designers, the automotive industry, beverage companies (water bottles were a previous job), wineries, breweries, and more to create experiences, spaces, and products that satisfy every sense. "When you think about all the senses, everything is always on," he says. "We know we're not doing good work when people start to complain. I'm doing my best work when no one really knows that it's being done."

The Sonoma County native grew up around breweries like Lagunitas and loads of wineries, in time attending the University of California, Davis. The chemistry major explored brewing and winemaking classes, doing extracurricular research on the local liquids. "If something is produced in my backyard and is sold all over the world, I've got to know a little bit about it," he says. The collected knowledge proved handy in 2011, right around the start of graduate school, when a filmmaker called.

Godfather director Francis Ford Coppola wanted someone to lead a truly blind tasting at his winery. Was Dr. Wedler interested? "When Francis Ford Coppola calls and asks you to do something, you kind of say yes," he says. "Then you get off the phone and realize what you got yourself into."

His Tasting in the Dark event series, since expanded to include beer, takes blindfolded attendees on an inner tour to rarely investigated lands—namely, their noses and mouths. Each event starts with the participants sniffing the surroundings, temporarily ignoring the beer or wine. "It sets a mood and sets a thought process." The ears come next. "What vibrates? What hums? What about the airflow? What do we hear going on outside?" Dr. Wedler asks. "You can never find anywhere that's completely silent."

Attendees then inhale the liquid's scent and discuss associations. Dr. Wedler likes placing aromas and flavors in the context of pleasurable and memorable foods. "When I smell a really hazy IPA, I think about the skin of jalapeño peppers," he says. It's specific, but specificity can help. "You're not crazy if you smell an IPA and say, 'Yeah, I smell pine resin, I smell stonefruit.' These things are real. The things that smell like peaches in peaches, might also make your beer smell [like] a peach. As an organic chemist, I can tell you a lot of these things have the same compounds. Nature has a way of making that happen."

Remember, Dr. Wedler was running these tastings while still attending UC Davis. He dreamed of teaching, a professorship to accompany his Accessible Science nonprofit, which runs hands-on chemistry camps for visually impaired children. People change. Upon graduating with a PhD in computational organic chemistry in 2017, he swapped a tenure-track academic future for startup life at Senspoint,

where the guiding viewpoint is this: Our eyes keep the world at arm's length, if not further. We need to look deeper.

"We can look at the moon, for crying out loud. It's the sense we use the most without thinking about it," he says. Eyesight is easy. You've likely had lots of practice. Our sense of hearing requires more intimacy, but a distance remains. Not so with touching, smelling, and tasting. They demand vulnerabilities and trust. "We're putting a part of something into ourselves," Dr. Wedler says. "That's the most vulnerable sense and the one that we focus on the least, and we're least literate in."

Beer becomes part of us, and then it leaves both body and mind. There's a buzz, there's friends, there's conversation, there's late-night pizza, there's . . . well, I'm not sure what was so memorable. "People often don't think beyond that pint," he says. "Friends make the experience, that's fine, but it's our job to be stewards of the industry and try to make beer that true experience. How can we think about beer, and think about beer as a lens to create moments that are not lost for years and years and years?"

You can answer that question with your eyes shut.

★ ★ ★

Advice: "I always tell people, Hey, look, beer, wine, whatever—they are subjective. They're art forms. You don't ask someone what painting you should hang on the wall. You just know what you like and what you don't."

—Dr. Henry "Hoby" Wedler, cofounder, Senspoint Design

★ ★ ★

DON'T FEEL OVERWHELMED

Be it a festival or a boisterous Friday night, there arrives a moment during every beer-drinking marathon when my tongue and nose clock out, flavors blurring together like a watercolor painting during a rainstorm. "We're not working overtime," they bemoan, totally overwhelmed by the taste tsunami.

It's time to take the sensory equivalent of a smoke break. "Our abilities to naturally recalibrate are pretty amazing. Our senses can pretty easily get overwhelmed, and can pretty easily recover as well," says Lerdahl, Ninkasi's sensory specialist. "Whether you're at a sensory panel or a beer festival, just wait a little while. Take deep breaths of regular fresh air."

And drink water. It'll rinse away lingering flavors and provide a hydration boost, always a good idea if you're getting after a couple of double IPAs or a peanut butter–packed stout. As for your nose, it can also short-circuit from so much sensory intake. "If you just stick your nose in there and keep smelling and

New Belgium Brewing sensory specialist Lindsay Barr helped create the DraughtLab app.

smelling and smelling and tasting and tasting and tasting, you're just going to desensitize yourself and it's going to become more difficult," Amato says.

Nasal fatigue is a real thing! Amato resets her olfactory system by smelling something different—namely, her arm. "I'll be at other judging competitions and see my fellow arm sniffers," she says, laughing. The idea is that you don't really smell like anything to yourself, so you're "cleansing" your nasal receptors with a neutral scent.

Some people swear by nibbling crackers between samples, or waving a coffee bean beneath their nose. But really, are you going to stuff Sumatra beans into your pocket before heading out for the night? You've got all the skin you need in the sensory game. Also, people *way* smarter than me are not big boosters for those approaches.

⭐ ⭐ ⭐

Fun Fact: Beer is so nice that we always smell it twice. The first method is by sniffing, shooting aromatic molecules up your nasal passageways and to your olfactory receptors. This is called orthonasal olfaction. The second way is retronasal olfaction: when you swallow, the odor molecules meander through your mouth and into your nasal cavity a second time, through a rear corridor, helping you perceive flavor as you exhale through your nose.

⭐ ⭐ ⭐

⭐ ⭐ ⭐

Advice: "Nine times out of ten, what needs to be reset is not your tasting instrument but your brain. That's what gets exhausted. When my brain gets overwhelmed, sometimes I'll take a sip of beer, keep it in my mouth, and start reading something or counting the tiles on the ceiling. In these moments, if I've managed to distract myself, the flavors will pop right out."

—Mirella Amato, Master Cicerone, *Beerology* author

⭐ ⭐ ⭐

"I'm not really a big fan of the cracker or the coffee bean. I think they kind of bring your senses to a level that's not very accurate," says Lindsay Barr, New Belgium Brewing's sensory specialist. "I did do a study once to see if giving panelists crackers helps with fatigue. The answer is no. The quality of my data didn't go up with the insertion of the cracker."

Instead, the best practices are moderation and frequent intermissions. New Belgium limits tasting panels to eight samples, with at least a thirty-second break between beers and plenty of water at the ready. "Our panelists will very much tell us if we've gone overboard," Barr says. "We've gone up to ten, and then on the tenth sample, they're like, 'You might as well not use my data.'"

WHY YOU SHOULD DRINK LAGER, THE SUPERIOR BEER

Chris Lohring, founder and head brewer, Notch Brewing

★ ★ ★

Notch Brewing head brewer and founder Chris Lohring.

For craft beer novices seeking a safe place, IPAs provide easy shelter. They are consistently the highest-rated, most coveted beers and possess flavor intensities celebrated by experts, or at least the ones on social media. There is no risk in ordering an IPA or posting one on Instagram—you'll get likes everywhere you look. You're safe. You're also blindly following the herd.

Craft beer is suffocating at the hands of a narrow set of flavors and aromatics that appeal, to some degree, to the lowest common denominator. Who dislikes sweet and citrus? These profiles dominate modern beer because, quite frankly, they are familiar. What does a twelve-year-old enjoy? Sweet, fruit, candy—and that's not too far from today's IPA.

An honest brewer will tell you—that honest brewer being me—that lagers are superior in every which way, from the ingredients to the processes and skills required to produce them. Their beauty is their subtle-yet-sublime flavors and aromas, no intensities to be found. Talk to any brewer, and they'll tell you pilsner and pale lager sit at the summit of the

brewing craft. Over my twenty-five-year career, I've brewed everything from barley wines to hazy New England IPAs, but nothing gets me more excited to put on my boots than a twelve-hour day brewing a triple-decoction, 4 percent pilsner. It takes far more effort and expertise in the brewhouse to execute a pilsner than it does an IPA, and after twenty-five years I'm still refining and constantly seeking improvement.

Czech pilsner's flavors and aromatics are unfamiliar. Toast and biscuit, grass and pepper, bitter yet creamy: Kids don't crave these attributes when picking out breakfast in the cereal aisle. They are an acquired taste. Yet Czech pilsner's singular characteristics literally changed the entire beer world, acquiring legions of fans. Nearly 90 percent of the beer-drinking universe sips some variation on the crisp, golden, and refreshing lager. No other style, not even IPA (yet), has come close to matching Czech pilsner's influence.

I like beers that are not so obvious. The best evolve, open up, and let you discover nuances with temperature changes, or just by getting to know them better after a few rounds. Lagers deliver on these notes every time. Spend an hour with a liter of pilsner, and then try to do the same with an IPA. You'll understand that lager is your friend in beer. Here's a hashtag to keep you company: #lagerislife.

Matthew Davis is the sensory assistant and draft technician at Allagash Brewing.

MEET THE PANEL OF APPROVAL

Fridays are recycling day in my household, which also doubles as an impromptu workout. The blue plastic recycling bag bulges with bottles and cans, clinking, clanging, and crinkling as I struggle to tote the remains of the week to the curb.

My neighbors sometimes eye me with a peculiar mix of envy and, to be candid, concern. How can one human consume so much beer? How can he still cinch his jeans shut without the assistance of a stretchy bungee cord? Great questions! And my answer will be the *R* word: research. Look, getting drunk is easy. It's pretty cost-effective to ride the bottom-shelf vodka train to oblivion. I'm looking to make informed appraisals of beer, to see if a label's flavorful promise matches the carbonated reality. (Disappointments fast meet their drain-pour fate.)

I muse on more despondent nights that if journalism continues to collapse, maybe my Plan B career would be sitting on breweries' sensory panels. They're part of a broader quality-control program, measuring the human experience of a brewery's beer and ensuring that it pasts muster, time and again, and meets consumer expectation. "If you're used to buying a brand, you can have a reasonable expectation that if you [buy] a bottle from a store or you get a pint at a bar you'll have the same experience every time," says Lerdahl, who steers Ninkasi's sensory program.

This requires folks to be super finicky. "The function of the quality assurance program is to be a really fine-toothed comb and pick out small defects that may or may not be relevant to consumers but are a good indication of process deviations," says Barr, New Belgium's sensory specialist. "We're identifying various process issues that could eventually creep up and create consumer impact. If a beer fails a panel, it doesn't mean that we're immediately going to dump it. One of the things we always ask is, 'What is the consumer risk?'"

The risk is you and I will despise the beer, badmouth it, never buy it again, and leave disparaging reviews online and on social media. It's a scorched-earth policy that few can withstand in an era of unfettered choice. You may buy a beer once, but blahness means you won't buy it twice.

"Consumers are quite savvy. They can't always tell you there's diacetyl in the beer, but they can say they don't like it and it reminds them of cream or butter," Barr says. "They know what they're tasting. We don't give consumers enough credit. They're really quite good at tasting beer."

You're Good Enough, and Smart Enough, to Sit on a Sensory Panel

A brewery's sensory panelists are not all unicorns who can ID a skunky IPA from ten miles away. "They're interested in flavor and mindful about experiences," Barr says, noting that the best are beverage omnivores. "It takes somebody that's curious about what they're experiencing to be pretty good at attaching an experience with a sensory attribute. It takes time and practice."

She likes to train people by allowing them to draw on their emotions and experiences. "Sensory scientists tend to be really rigid in saying, 'This is the attribute and this is the language that you're going to use,'" Barr says. "But that really confines the panelists' vocabulary."

For example, if a beer reminds you of eating PB and J with your family in the summertime, say so. "Start with the analogy first," she says, "then you can draw from that emotion. OK, that's peanut butter, jelly, bread, toast, bread crusts. Then you can break those things apart into individual elements, standardize those terms, and then, if you want, assign chemical compounds."

This approach allows breathing room for beer's forever widening spectrum of flavor and fragrance.

★ ★ ★

Advice: "In beer, aroma is where you'll find the bulk of variation and are typically going to identify potential defects."

—Lindsay Barr, sensory specialist, New Belgium Brewing

★ ★ ★

A rigorous quality-control programs helps breweries ensure each batch of beer is perfect.

"We're throwing everything under the sun in beer," she says. "Beer is not just light lager anymore, so we need a broader vocabulary to describe attributes."

Sensory panels are not tests requiring you to cover your answers with a crooked elbow, lest someone steal them. Panelists are encouraged to converse. "I ask our panelists to casually discuss the flavors of our beers and what makes our IPAs different from one another. What is *your* experience with this beer? Something might resonate with somebody that, for instance, didn't recognize the green tea characteristics in Glütiny [New Belgium's gluten-reduced pale ale]."

That's to be expected. We all have different sensitivities, aromatic turn-ons and turn-offs. (Don't cook salmon in my apartment if you'd like to remain my friend.) Tasting beer as a group and listening to

★ ★ ★

Advice: "The best thing anyone can do to develop their palate and judging abilities is to taste with more experienced tasters."

—Mirella Amato, Master Cicerone, *Beerology* author

★ ★ ★

others' descriptions can be instructive, helping you recognize your strengths and weaknesses. "It's not one golden taster making the decisions," Lerdahl says. "Even the most highly trained people can have blindnesses, a day where they're sick, or strong personal opinions."

So would I be a worthy sensory panelist at a brewery? There's one way to find out for certain.

A Quality Trip: Spending the Day inside Allagash's Sensory Program

It's a soaking fall morning in Portland, Maine, plump raindrops beating a rapid rhythm on the roof of Allagash Brewing, where I'm sitting in the taproom and staring at a flight of beer.

This is not the first time I've drunk beer at nine o'clock in the morning, but it is the most solemn. I'm participating in Allagash's twice-weekly field quality panel, one of fifteen or so people assessing the integrity of beers that have departed the brewery, awaiting customers' final judgment at stores and bars.

Around me, employees silently swirl, sniff, and sip samples to decide whether each beer hits its flavor target, or whether there's a specific fault, perhaps present, perhaps introduced. "We always spike beers with different off flavors," sensory assistant

Allagash Brewing's headquarters in Portland, Maine.

Sampling batches of White, a Belgian-inspired witbier, at Allagash Brewing.

and draft technician Matthew Davis explains, handing me a laminated list of flavor attributes such as 4-ethyl phenol, responsible for horse sweat and burnt plastic. How many beers were spiked? "That changes too."

I ponder my sample of White, the brewery's flagship witbier, which should taste slightly sweet and sour, mildly bitter, and faintly of minerals. "Tastes overly harsh," I write in the iPad set up with sensory software from DraughtLab, which collects data on panelists' impressions. (See page 100 for more on DraughtLab.) "Too astringent." I move on to the Belgian-style Tripel, a beer evocative of honey, bubble gum, grapes, and green apples. "There is a sourness I

don't love," I write. The coffee-infused James Bean, a tripel aged in bourbon barrels, has a "drying sourness that turns me off," while the smoothly malty House Beer hits its pear and grapefruit notes.

Wow, that was a lot of flawed beer, I think, returning my tray and walking over to a table to receive my reward—candy corn or gummy bears—and the answer: only the Tripel was adulterated, dosed with the acetic acid that I identified as sour. How were my taste buds so wrong? "Sensory is really humbling," Davis tells me. "Putting into words why you like or dislike things is hard."

For breweries, so is making sure that beer tastes the same every single day, no matter where it's

A peek inside part of Allagash Brewing's wood cellar, where beers patiently age.

bought or sold, no flaws to be found. That's why I'm spending the day at Allagash. It's one of America's premier breweries, delivering beer guaranteed to be damn good, no matter whether it's a spontaneously fermented wild beer, a rustic saison, or a stout gone silky with oats. I'll buy Allagash beer anywhere and everywhere, largely because the brewery operates an airtight quality-control program. The field quality panel is part of a battery of tests to ensure that you're not drinking imperfect beer. It's a scientific dance of analyzing grains, monitoring yeast strains, checking on carbonation levels, and running rigorous sensory panels, like the next one on my day's aromatic agenda.

All the White Moves

I'm led to the break room, which is filled with bins of breakfast cereals, a refrigerator bearing a picture of famous singer Cher—it's the Cher'd Fridge!— and beer taps pumping out Allagash White. Though it's still on the south side of noon, I'm poured a full glass and instructed to drink. "It's a warm-up beer to cleanse your palate," creative manager Mat Trogner tells me. I follow marching orders as he escorts me up a set of stairs and into an austere room crammed with cramped cubicles too small to extend both your arms. I sit down at one and a small door in front of me slides open,

like the sort used to feed misbehaving prison inmates in movies.

"I'll take that," says Karl Arnberg, Allagash's sensory program manager, removing my glass of White. He passes me three small samples of lightly hazy liquid, each one topped with a black plastic disc, and a piece of paper. It's the brewery's true-to-target test, evaluating acceptability while taking into account seasonal variability—year over year, no two crops of grains or hops will be identical. It's my job to figure out whether these samples hit the target for five metrics: appearance, aroma, flavor, mouthfeel, and overall.

This isn't a sensory deprivation chamber; it's a sensory *amplification* chamber. I try to parse each sample's individual components, doing my best to discern defects. I decide that sample 872 is too astringent and unbalanced, while 149 is slightly puckering. Then there's 966, smelling like an overripe banana that's lingered on a kitchen counter too long. After the test, I meet Arnberg in a nearby office and relay my findings, proud to have helped defend drinkers from subpar Allagash White. Interestingly, samples 149 and 872 were flawless and, in fact, the same beer. "It's a combination that I use often with guests and new tasters to show when they are overly critical," Arnberg says. "It's a good demonstration [of] how subjective sensory is at its core. It's an uphill battle to train tasters to not only be accurate but consistent with their feedback."

Allagash Brewing sensory assistant and draft technician Matthew Davis pours a beer sample for testing.

Furthermore, just because 149 and 872 were tamper-free doesn't mean they were guaranteed to pass muster. I could potentially find something outside the accepted flavor profile. "Those are the experimental tests of the panel," Arnberg says. "We ask the tasters to tell us if they are correct or incorrect as examples of the brand." In the case of 966, he says, the sample was spiked with elevated levels of ethyl butyrate, a compound responsible for that fruity fragrance I identified.

"It's actually a really good sign of fresh beer," Arnberg says. Ethyl butyrate fades with time, but at present concentrations, it did not fit Allagash White's sensory profile. I ask Arnberg why, time and again, I've proved to be a hypercritical Debbie Downer, discovering negativities where none exist. "It's always easy to look for something," he says. It's tougher to applaud the positive or, better yet, ensure a beer matches the status quo.

I shouldn't be so hard on myself. Arnberg trains panelists on twenty-nine distinct flavor attributes, a process that takes two to three months. "We're creating a mosaic of opinion," he says. This might seem like overkill or even a waste. Why not just send beer through some contraption equipped with a mechanical nose? Analytical machines only provide concentrations of aromas and flavors, he says, but without context. Humans need to put those numbers into the realm of the beer and provide a yes-no range for each chemical flavor, for each brand, from first sniff to last sip. "We have all the sensory abilities of machines, but [we also have] the intelligence to put all the numbers together," Arnberg says.

Off to the Lab

Safe in the knowledge that there's at least *one* job robots will not steal from humankind, I head to the lab to meet microbiologist and head of quality control Zach Bodah. The lab and its staff serve as the brewery's first and last line of defense, propagating the yeast used to ferment most Allagash beers. The organisms are stored in a small freezer with a thermostat kept at a nippy negative eighty degrees Celsius. Bodah opens the freezer door and displays stacked white boxes filled with frosty vials, a party just waiting to begin. "We have enough yeast to last 25 years," Bodah says.

Moreover, the lab team serves as the brewery's microbial safety guards. They ensure that bacteria and yeast remain in their respective lanes, no small task in a brewery that gleefully plays with *Brettanomyces*, a feral creature that, given the chance, will happily squat in any barrel, tank, or batch of beer. "*Brettanomyces* likes to live in porous wood," Bodah says, not a small worry in this very, very wood-focused brewery.

Also cause for concern: too little or too much carbonation. Bottle conditioning, in which beer is naturally carbonated, is a sensitive and complex beast. Ever had a bottle that gushed like a geyser upon opening? I have. I've also had bottles explode inside my fridge, sending glass shards shooting into my leftover salad, as well as bottles pop their caps as I drove sixty-five on the interstate. They sounded like a gunshot, nearly causing me to swerve my car off the road, sending me to an uncertain date with a ditch.

Bodah's staff ensures that bottles have the right level of fizz, preventing both explosive situations and the disappointment of flat beer. Each bottle's carbonation levels are dialed in tighter than a radio signal, not only upon departing Allagash but also throughout their life-span in the marketplace. "Consumer safety is our top concern," he says.

I walk back to the taproom to find a lunchtime crowd clinking glasses of White, not a care in the world except, maybe, wondering who will grab the next round. A brewery's quality-control program is the invisible hand ensuring consumer happiness. The only surprises are the flavors that are supposed to be present, not the accidental ones.

Making beer is easy. Making great beer is hard. Making great beer backed by the bulletproof promise of grade-A quality, that's the toughest challenge of all. Even more than drinking beer at nine o'clock in the morning.

> **BREWED AWAKENING:** "The first time I went to a bar in Belgium called the Kulminator"—the Antwerp bar is one of the world's finest repositories of Belgian beer—"was an eye-opener. At the time, the beer selection was insane. The beer menu looked like a phone book, and they had beers from 1974 until today. It was like going into the home of an older Belgian couple that had the craziest beer selection in the world."
>
> —Mikkel Borg Bjergsø, owner, Mikkeller

GIVE AMBERS A FRESH LOOK

★ ★ ★

"Many pioneering craft breweries focused on amber ales. To me, that's a style that's very well balanced, with a combination of malt and hop character. Now amber ales are a style that is pretty far back in the rearview mirror," says Master Cicerone Ryan Daley. It's time to make these objects appear a little bit closer. "They still have a lot of aroma and flavor complexity, but at the same time are pretty easy drinking. They appeal to both sides—somebody that is a little farther along in the sensory abilities, as well as somebody that's just coming into beer or isn't used to intense flavor profiles. In terms of what you get from the experience, it's tough to beat." Here are three widely available ambers to help color a new opinion:

1. Anderson Valley Brewing: Boont Amber Ale. Two kinds of crystal malts create the crimson hue in this complex California classic that smells of toffee and fresh-baked raisin cookies.

2. Left Hand Brewing: Sawtooth Ale. Formerly the Colorado brewery's flagship, Sawtooth still appeals with its balance of bready malt and herbal bitterness.

3. Tröegs Independent Brewing: HopBack Amber Ale. The Pennsylvanians use a hopback device to recirculate fruity and floral Crystal and resinous Nugget hops through the caramel-rich ale.

You'll be better off red with a glass of Tröegs HopBack Amber Ale.

THE APP-SOLUTELY BEST WAY TO PERFORM SENSORY

★ ★ ★

In an idealized world, breweries of every conceivable scale would run a robust sensory program, squadrons of well-trained panelists ready to identify off flavors at the drop of a hop. Here's the not-so-rosy reality: the majority of breweries produce less than one thousand barrels of beer a year, employees and resources stretched thinner than a baby's hair.

"There are very few companies where you have the numbers, time, and expertise to put an actual sensory scientist at the helm," says New Belgium sensory specialist Lindsay Barr. As for the software available to the average brewery, most of it was too expensive and too complicated, she says, requiring a sensory scientist to decode the data. It's tough to sip from a glass full of so much irony.

"It was a gap in the industry that I almost immediately recognized," Barr says. As a remedy, she partnered with fellow sensory experts and software designers to create DraughtLab. It's an intuitive, functional, and, as I learned at Allagash, easy-to-use app designed to help breweries create a blueprint for a beer brand's description. "If it's

not written down, if it's not documented, how are you really going to understand if you have any flavor drift?" she asks.

For drinkers like you and me, the app is also a solid instructive tool and an illustrative look at the data a brewery is looking to measure. From foam quantity to carbonation and aroma, DraughtLab provides an exhaustive list of sensory prompts paired with potential descriptions (fatty! umami! metallic!) compiled into this pretty map that we've placed on the following page (draughtlab.com).

CONSISTENCY IS NOT A FOUR-LETTER WORD

They seem so very long ago, those days I regularly drank the same beer twice. A bottle needn't grip me at first sip. I could get to know a beer's charms over the course of 12 ounces, then 24, and finally 72, the boozy multiplication rooted in a formulaic certainty: breweries' flagship beer would never let me down, as dependable as those college friendships that, decades on, I still hold near and dear.

Stalwarts such as Sierra Nevada Pale Ale, New Belgium Fat Tire, Widmer Brothers Hefeweizen, and Brooklyn Lager had recipes refined with practice and time, and lots of it. I knew what I was getting, until I stopped getting them. I grew disloyal and settled into one-off relationships with an endless series of fruited this, dry-hopped that, soured whatever. I craved more, more, more to fill a hole of curiosity that could never be filled, no matter how many beers I consumed. And that's the rub about being a promiscuous beer drinker: there's never enough.

I mistook quantity for quality, something I should've known firsthand. If I write a dozen stories in a week, there's no way they'll all be journalistic gems. Wedding creativity to consistency is tough on tight deadlines, accelerated by our fickle culture's ferocious thirst for the new. Nowadays beer need only taste good, or at least interesting, but once before brewers move on to another recipe, the old one discarded like spent grain, the formula for success the new and next. There is beauty in reliable quality, a brewery that can

Jane Killebrew, Anheuser-Busch InBev's global vice president of brewing and quality.

consistently nail a blemish-free recipe. Of late, I've found myself sailing back to the flagships docked in the beer aisle such as Sierra Nevada, particularly its Pale Ale. Like a best friend, it'll never let you down and remains compelling company.

"When I first tasted a dusty bottle of Sierra Nevada Pale Ale that had somehow made its way to the northeast of Scotland, it completely blew my mind," says BrewDog cofounder James Watt. "The explosion of tropical fruits, citrus, pine, and resin was like nothing I'd ever tasted. I didn't know beer could taste like that."

In a world that's always changing, it's nice that some things never change, a beer tasting so nice you want to drink it twice. Aren't you jazzed about dependability? No? I understand, and so does Jane Killebrew, Anheuser-Busch InBev's gloriously named global vice president of brewing and quality.

"Consistency can be deemed as being incredibly average, right? It means that you perform the same every time," she says. "Developing a new product is an incredibly exciting thing to do, but that's not the most challenging thing I do. The most challenging thing I do is to repeat it every single time."

Whether they're served in Alaska or Argentina, and whether or not you dig their taste, beers like Budweiser and Bud Light will be flavor photocopies. It's the product of a multilevel, globally integrated fail-safe procedure refined for decades. "When I started more than three decades ago, we brewed Bud in maybe a half dozen places," Killebrew says. Today's count is sixty-five, from North America to Europe, Brazil, and South Africa, and growing every year. "It gets interesting when you brew with ingredients that are variable," she says.

Too much or too little rain can affect hop and barley crops' health, yield, and nutrients, altering yeast's performance. "Yeast is a living organism. It has a mind of its own," Killebrew explains. "One of the most challenging things is that you don't know what you don't know." To crack nature's annually shifting

code, the company's Saint Louis pilot brewery runs numerous raw material tests, brewing ten-barrel batches of Budweiser to decipher crop characteristics. "It helps us get a head start on any adjustments," Killebrew says.

Monthly, the company flies in samples of every global Budweiser, a four-day gauntlet of blind samples, eighteen at a time, poured identically and served at equal temperatures. The samples are assessed to ensure unwavering sameness. "The consumer's job is to figure out which blueprint they love, and our job is to go deliver the blueprint every single time."

Think about dining at your favorite restaurant. You want—no, you demand—that your favorite pasta dish be prepared exactly the same on every visit. Deviation equals disappointment, no second chances for a new chef. "Sometimes I feel boring when I go to a restaurant and order the same thing every time, but whenever I stray I'm disappointed," Killebrew says.

For breweries of all scales and approaches, the task is a note-for-note re-creation of the original. Adhering to a recipe and processes will never go as viral as novel formulation, but it's critical to a brewery's enduring success. It takes a minute to create, a lifetime to re-create. "You've given a customer an expectation of what the beer should be. It's our job to deliver that expectation every time," Killebrew says. "This flavor-match never stops. It's about ensuring the consistency of the beer for eternity."

An ad for Wild Basin Boozy Sparkling Water from Oskar Blues Brewery.

A HARD TURN FROM BEER

Platform Beer Company rarely lets its brewing equipment rest. Across its five locations in 2018, the company produced more than 200 different fermented beverages, ranging from blueberry ciders to coffee-infused pale ales and creamy IPAs.

"We've built a customer base that was not only okay with us innovating, but they were almost expecting it," says Paul Benner, a founder of the fast-expanding Cleveland, Ohio, company that opened in 2014.

Platform even produces LaCroix with a kick. Its Seltzer Project line of alcoholic hard seltzers features flavors like tangerine-grapefruit and strawberry-lemonade, canned at a crushable 5 percent ABV. For consumers, this creates a linguistic quandary: What do you call a brewery that makes beer, cider, boozy seltzer, and more? "Beer is our core, but I'd be lying if we didn't think of ourselves as an innovative beverage company," Benner says.

"A decade ago, we just talked about the beer drinker versus the wine drinker versus the spirits drinker," says Danelle Kosmal, a vice president of Nielsen's beverage alcohol practice. "That no longer exists. It's just a beverage drinker now."

New Brands Bubble Up

Increasingly, the see-through sparkler—typically made by fermenting sugar—has become the bubbly plaything of breweries. And new entrants to the space are piling up, including Kentucky's Braxton Brewing and its Vive

Hard Seltzer, Florida's M.I.A. Beer Company, makers of HRD WTR, Boston Beer Company, the producers of Samuel Adams beer and Truly Hard Seltzer, not to mention Twisted Tea, Angry Orchard cider, Tura Alcoholic Kombucha, and (phew!) Wild Leaf, a "craft hard tea."

The synergies make sense to Maura Hardman. She's the PR and marketing manager for Washington State's Two Beers Brewing, whose sister brands are Seattle Cider Company and Sound Craft Seltzer, made from organic sugar and produce.

"It was an easy, natural progression because we already have a brewery," Hardman says. "We have the institutional knowledge."

Moreover, these breweries are operating in a climate of permissiveness that didn't exist when Barack Obama was president. In 2014, the Brewers

Seattle's Two Beers Brewing makes Sound Craft Seltzer.

Association revised its guidelines to allow for brewers using corn and rice. This wasn't the definition's final form. At the end of 2018, the trade group also nixed the decree that required brewers to mostly make beer. The fermented playing field was officially wide open.

Absence of Rule(s)

I've long adhered to a personal business philosophy I call the Table of Twenty Legs. Each one represents a client. If one or two vanish, enough remain to keep my career upright. Breweries are no different. Beer brands' lifespan has become truncated. Gone are the days of nurturing a beer such as Sierra Nevada Pale Ale from infancy into a healthy adulthood, remaining as ageless, relevant, and lucrative as a movie star. New beers appear and disappear in the time it took you to read this sentence.

So welcome to beverage world, where a single brewery might meet all your liquid needs, one that might look something like Oskar Blues. The Colorado-born company began with beer but its associated divisions sell soda, coffee, canned cocktails, and hard seltzer, not to mention bicycles and even wedding packages at REEB Ranch, its North Carolina property.

"Oskar Blues has always been a lifestyle brand," says Matt Fraser, the president and chief operating officer of the CANarchy Craft Brewery Collective, of which Oskar Blues is a member. And lifestyles forever evolve. I'm no longer that 19-year-old sneaking Genesee Cream Ale longnecks inside my college dive, then spasm-dancing to ska. People change. Breweries do too.

A GROWING RELATIONSHIP: BREWERS TEAM UP WITH HOP FARMERS

Something was off with the scent of those Citra and Mosaic hops. North Carolina's Burial Beer regularly used the two varieties in its IPAs, Mosaic lending lovely blueberry panache, Citra its punch bowl of tropical fruit. But certain batches of the prior year's cultivars brought to mind less-savory descriptors. To Burial cofounder Doug Reiser, the Mosaic hops were reminiscent of diesel and onions, while the Citra hops suggested artificial fruit—you know, Creamsicles.

"They were much different hops," Reiser says. "Last year we had moments like, Man, these are shitty hops. I don't know what to do." Burial's

solutions: Adding hops on the hot side of the brewing process, mostly lending bitterness, as well as to its mixed-fermentation beers. Secondly, pursue greater control over hop sourcing.

"We wanted to work with a broker who would let us learn about the origin of the hops that we were buying and work with small farms that we knew were highly regarded for growing specific varietals," says Reiser, whose brewery began sourcing Mosaic hops from Champoux Farms in Washington's Yakima Valley. According to Reiser, Champoux's Mosaic "was bright blueberry and pineapple purée and such a wonderful fruity hop."

Burial is one of a growing number of breweries forging closer ties with hop farmers across the US,

Don't you just want to dive headlong into this heap of fresh hops? If only my publishers sprung for scratch and sniff on this page.

Germany, and New Zealand, seeking transparency about an agrarian product that's often opaque to the buyer. Unlike chefs, most brewers can't hit a farmers' market to eyeball, smell, and select the choicest hops. Typically, breweries buy them from middlemen—wholesalers and brokers whose products are a blend of crops culled from different farms, varying quality levels, and sensory profiles merged into a homogenized whole.

Sixpoint Brewery founder Shane Welch calls it "hop sausage," and he's no fan. "You need to identify the parameters of hops," Welch says. "Just because it's called Citra, it's not good enough."

Think of hops like ripening fruit. A peak strawberry balances juicy sweetness and acidity, while overripe berries are mushy, sugary, and fragrant. Hop characteristics also evolve during maturation. Picked early, Simcoe suggests passionfruit, peach, and guava; let Simcoe linger too long on a bine and it'll express garlic and onion. Take into account the huge acreage that farms are planting to meet demand for varieties such as Citra (more than 6,000 additional acres in 2018), and the logistical and aromatic challenge will start to come into focus.

"It's literally impossible to run the thresher, pelletizer, and picking machines for 100 percent of the acres during that window where hops are at peak flavor," Welch says. "That's the bind we're in."

Around five years ago, Welch began breaking free of the established system by traveling to the Pacific Northwest and Germany, building relationships with hop growers one handshake at a time. "It had to be done through old-school networking. You go there and talk to someone," Welch says. And the proof is in the pilsner: The Crisp is thrillingly spicy and floral, crammed with choice German Tettnang and Hallertau hops personally selected by Sixpoint. (The brewery also champions growers in its Farm to Pint series highlighting hops from a single estate, such as Toppen-ish IPA, made from Cornerstone Ranches' candied-orange El Dorado and resinous Centennial hops.)

Vermont's Hill Farmstead is regarded as one of the world's elite breweries, masters of hop-forward beers and more. Sometime around 2014 or 2015, though, founder Shaun Hill had an epiphany. "I realized that we were trying to make great, consistent beer, and the greatest variable was the fact that we were just opening a box of hops and we knew nothing about its contents," he says.

Over the next few years, Hill pursued his own links with farmers to nix the rogue variable from his brewing equation. In early 2016, he flew to New Zealand to discuss a hop-growing project with a friend and, fortuitously, happened upon a hop farm recently bought by an American investment group. Freestyle Farms, as the estate was later rebranded, grew some of Hill's favorite varietals, including white wine–like Nelson Sauvin and lemon-limey Motueka.

For most American brewers, connecting directly with farmers on the other side of the world was impossible; a grower-owned cooperative oversaw sales,

Sorting through recently harvested hops can be hands-on work.

Working the hop fields during harvest.

championing New Zealand varieties rather than individual producers, terroir be damned. Freestyle offered Hill Farmstead and a handful of other breweries a rare opportunity: Fly to New Zealand and select your own Southern Hemisphere hops.

Earlier this year, Hill completed his first selection of Motueka and Nelson Sauvin hops. Face time with farmers let Hill discuss his ideal characteristics, a conversation less common than you might assume. "Hops have just been harvested when the farmer was ready and not necessarily based upon when the brewer was happy about them," says Hill, who now critically selects nearly all of his hops, including German and Pacific Northwest varieties.

This shifts standard operating procedure. Historically, choosing hops was a privilege for large breweries with immense buying power. Industrial breweries have had a huge hand in dictating what hops are grown, mainly favoring varieties that deliver bitterness, not aroma or flavor. Hops were a commodity. America's modern brewing revolutionaries, however, craved cultivars that delivered memorable fragrances, a Cascade (hop) effect that ushered in the modern era of citrus and pine.

Perceptive hop farmers saw an opportunity to build a new business model. By 2009, the Yakima Valley's Segal Ranch had dwindled to 83 acres of hops, down from 470. To save the family business, third-generation farmer John Segal Jr. started pitching hops to breweries like Captain Lawrence and Russian River, inviting them to his Washington farm for a hands-on lesson in the quality of his hops, dried at lower temperatures to produce an intense perfume.

"I tell folks, 'Once you rub our hops at our farm, you will know the quality we have,'" Segal says, noting their flagship "high-oil Cascades" that pop with grapefruit peel. "Once brewers come to our farm, walk around and see the operation, they get it." Now back up to 470 acres, Segal Ranch's top-end client list includes Other Half, Lagunitas, Odell, Industrial Arts, and more. "This whole approach saved our farm," Segal says. "If I hadn't done this, we would've gone out of business. Period."

In a perfect world, all brewers would select their hops according to a harvest window, but that level of control is impossible. Mother Nature works faster than picking machines and, moreover, most farms are not set up for direct-to-brewery sales, even if there were fewer than 7,000 of them vying for this fragile ingredient. But as the industry continues to mature, look for discerning breweries to prioritize hops that are best suited for their beers, not just settling for what's available.

"I feel we're at a point in our life where we should be able to select our lots," says Reiser, who's standing his ground by understanding what's in the ground. "Terroir matters."

Workers at Segal Ranch in Grandview, Washington, harvest hops.

DRINKING DESTINATION

The Pacific Northwest: Where Fresh-Hop Beers Are Fall's Fleeting Specialty

Jeff Alworth, author, *The Beer Bible*

★ ★ ★

In the breweries of the Pacific Northwest, late August is an exciting time. The hop bines that grow the nation's commercial crop are near harvest then, and brewers prepare for a special seasonal beer. They consult with the growers daily, waiting for the moment of perfect ripeness (each variety will mature at a slightly different rate). When the day arrives, breweries dispatch trucks to the fields and fire up their mash tuns. Within hours, the trucks will return with freshly picked but undried hops ("fresh hops") that they infuse into boiling wort. It is the most anticipated time of the brewing calendar, and the following six weeks constitute a bacchanal that rivals the release of French Beaujolais nouveau, a young wine made from harvest grapes, in local excitement.

Conventional hops are dried immediately after harvest to lock in the freshness of the essential oils that give beer its flavors, aromas, and bitterness. But

(continued on next page)

After harvest, brewers carefully analyze and select their favored lots of hops.

After picking, hops are quickly processed to preserve their aromatics.

they also change the flavors of those oils as surely as drying changes basil. A floral, lightly grapefruity dried Cascade hop, for example, smells like a blossoming orange orchard, with jammy, mandarin flavors when fresh. The beers that result are unlike any made with conventional hops.

They are, unfortunately, incredibly evanescent. The compounds that give fresh hops their zing are volatile, and they start dissipating shortly after the beer is made. They're at their peak just briefly and will ebb in intensity within days of that moment. A beer at perfection one week will have lost some life a week later. Fresh hop beers must therefore be served extremely fresh, almost certainly on tap, and drunk as quickly as possible.

And yet fresh hop season is so much fun precisely because it's no more predictable than wildflower season in the Cascades. Hundreds of breweries make these beers, which begin filtering onto the market in mid- to late September, and fans flood breweries and pubs

Fun Fact: Breakside Brewing often flash-freezes fresh hops with liquid nitrogen and shatters them, cracking open the lupulin glands and releasing resins and oils. The process creates deeply fragrant fresh hop beers. (For a look at the techniques, see page 72).

The Beer Bible author Jeff Alworth.

to track down examples that are at the peak of freshness. Some breweries have become known for their prowess with these beers—Breakside, Bale Breaker, Deschutes—but spectacular examples may come from anywhere. The hops express the character of the field, and even a beer made the same way a year later will taste different. Savvy drinkers know to cast their nets wide.

By October, it's difficult to find a pub that doesn't have one on tap—in many cases they'll account for a quarter or third of the tap list. Then, before locals have had a chance to tire of these vivid flavors, they begin to disappear. By mid-October fresh hop beers will become rare, and sightings are passed around like rumors on social media. By Halloween, when the last are gone, there can be a lingering melancholy among pubgoers—but it's exactly the longing that revives again the following autumn and creates such excitement here. Fresh hop season is truly one of the marvels of the annual beer calendar, and every beer drinker should make a trip to the Northwest some early October to experience it firsthand.

Advice: "As a kid, I played games where I would do blind tastings of food and I had to guess what I was eating. My sister and I had a babysitter who would go into our pantry or fridge and take out little bits of this and that. We'd sit there with our eyes closed and hold it in our hands. We'd smell it, taste it, feel it, and try to guess what it was. I do that to people all the time now, too."

—Jules Lerdahl, sensory specialist, Ninkasi Brewing

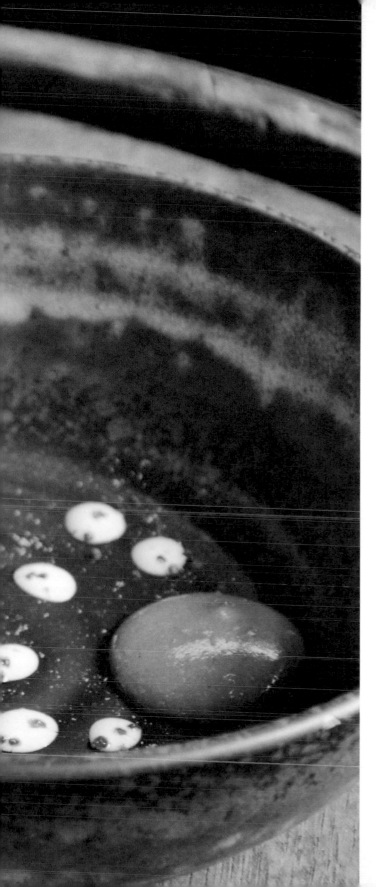

EAT THESE WORDS

THE NEW WORLD OF FOOD AND BEER PAIRINGS

Once upon a time, in a New York City not so long ago, my roommates and I regularly left our Brooklyn apartment around nine or ten o'clock on Saturday nights to hit downtown-Manhattan dive bars where canned beer was sold cold, cheap, and till four o'clock in the morning. Last call was a blurred badge of pride, the coming sunrise an affirmation that we were squeezing all the juice out of the Big Apple—or, you know, we were twenty-two.

How'd we do it? Pizza. There was a steady intake of steaming slices folded in half and consumed, like prescribed medicine, every couple of hours. Food served as ballast to keep us upright as we sloshed through the dark night.

As I aged, I went out earlier, went to bed earlier, and started revising my relationship to beer and food. Five-course beer dinners whetted my appetite for pairings at the dinner table, not hunched over on a street corner, pizza grease dripping on the sidewalk. I started toting Saison Dupont to Thanksgiving dinner, a peppery farmhouse ale that carves through gravy but rarely overwhelms salad. I sipped IPAs with Indian curries, schwarzbiers with hamburgers, smoked porters with beef stew, ESBs with fish and chips. Beer and food sang in easy harmony, a song I learned to play by heart.

Over time, beer dinners slowly turned into cover tunes, with couplings such as chocolaty imperial stouts with chocolate cake, lemony Berliner weisses with oysters. Brewpubs mostly played a deep-fried score of jalapeño poppers and saucy chicken wings, menus static since hair metal days. But new pairings trade jazzlike improvisation for greatest-hits execution—carrot cake and IPA, anyone?

> **BREWED AWAKENING:** "It all started when I was living in Los Angeles in the 1990s, which was during the pre-dawn years of craft beer. There were only a handful of breweries in L.A. and nothing compared to the ubiquity of craft breweries today. I was pulled into craft beer by Steps, a 'yuppie' bar across the street from the law firm where I worked as a paralegal. It served industrial-strength macro lagers, but they also carried Redhook ESB. In its heavy brown bottle, with a unique label that I had never seen the likes of, it looked and felt different. The beer was full-flavored, rich in malt character, and had a hop bitterness unlike anything I had tasted. It was startling."
>
> —Shaun "Sully" O'Sullivan, cofounder and brewmaster, 21st Amendment Brewery

Beer and food have once more been remixed. Brewpubs are winning Michelin stars and embracing a diverse epicurean approach, serving dim sum alongside Belgian beer. Breweries are ripping up restaurant menus and serving food every bit as thoughtful, and modern, as their beer. The best pairings offer a renewed playfulness and flavorful deviance. Ever pondered a cherry sour with Norwegian salmon?

None of this is overly complicated gastronomy. From painting bread with peanut butter and jelly to smoothing out dark coffee with rich milk, finding like-minded flavor matches is something we do naturally. We eat to live, and live to drink up life. Here's how to enhance your best eating-and-drinking you.

NO TIME FOR DINNER

Beer dinners once presented a premise familiar to fans of pleasure cruises: Diners would set sail on a three-hour tour across oceans of flavor, charting a course for three, four, five, or nine courses or more. The celebrations served as winding explorations of wonder, helping beer bob on the same level as wine.

I loved attending beer dinners, treating them as palatable lesson plans on the principles of pairing. By flickering candlelight I learned that lambic's acidity served as a cleansing counterpoint to rich and salty charcuterie, and that funky washed-rind cheeses went wild for *Brettanomyces*-fermented beers. I devoted mounds of minutes to devouring these invaluable nuggets of wisdom. Time, though, slowly became more valuable. Who could pledge three hours and one hundred dollars for a Thursday-night feast? It's an affliction of a digital era in which phones advertise an endless smorgasbord of nightly entertainment options, FOMO free of charge.

"In my experience, restaurants in the last five years have been like, 'Let's do a happy hour,'" says Sam Calagione, the founder and president of Dogfish Head Craft Brewery. Pairing knowledge could be served in a more casual, bite-size format tailored to our time-crunched, attention-arrested era. The new format meant people "don't need to sit down for a five-hour course with you and commit a whole night."

Calagione might be American brewing's best barometer for the state of beer and food. In 1995, he founded the Dogfish Head Brewing and Eats brewpub in coastal Delaware as a brewery burrowed inside a restaurant, committing to making the majority of its beers with culinary ingredients. "We intentionally had an open kitchen without a freezer so food and beer lovers could see us moving fresh ingredients out of that kitchen in one direction, on plates, and in another direction in five-gallon buckets and trays, whether it was maple syrup, pumpkin meat, or brown sugar, for beer," he says.

Dogfish Head started distributing beer in the late 1990s, providing restaurants and bars with sell sheets that touted the pairing potential of its beers with cheese, entrées, and chocolate—entire meals accompanied by beer, from appetizer to dessert. Calagione personally spread the pairing gospel at hundreds of beer dinners, his enthusiasm infectious, his reasoning sound and playful.

A flight accompanies a wide array of gastronomic options at Wolf's Ridge Brewing's dining room.

Here's an example: "Wine kind of hops around on the one leg of grapes while beer struts around elegantly on at least the two flavor legs of barley and hops, but then you can add yeast, herbs and spices," he says.

"Just by virtue of ingredient complexity, there's an opportunity to pair with more foods."

Great imagery, but you don't need a curated dinner to take a stroll around your brain with a beer.

Lessons are everywhere, pairings Googled on your computer or phone. "I'd say the excitement and interest in pairing beer and food has never been higher, but the situations have evolved."

A FOUR-PACK OF BEER-PAIRING ADVICE FROM DOGFISH HEAD FOUNDER SAM CALAGIONE

★ ★ ★

Most surprising pairing: "A piping-hot ballpark frank and a super-cold industrial light lager. Eat and drink them very quickly before the beer warms up and the frank cools down. Because neither one works at all at room temperature."

Most unlikely pairing: "Spicy butter chicken and Dogfish Head Namaste White or any Belgian white beer. You would think IPAs paired with Indian food would be the sweet-spot pairing, but a sweeter, fruitier lower-ABV beer like a Belgian-style white tamps down the spice with grace and aplomb."

Most fail-proof pairing: "A big, bold roasty stout like North Coast Old Rasputin, Victory Storm King, or Dogfish Head World Wide with a bar of artisanal, super-dark dark chocolate."

Most memorable pairing: "I had homemade chicha [a South American beer made with corn that's chewed, spit out, and fermented] paired with fire pit-roasted big larva in Ecuador last year. In the moment this pairing was delicious, but the local bacteria in the food and drink ended up agreeing to disagree with my constitution. I spent the night on my knees praying to the local porcelain gods."

Dogfish Head founder Sam Calagione.

PAIRINGS HEAD HOME

New York City is a land of glorious gastronomic excess. Given unlimited funds, or a freewheeling attitude toward credit cards, I could spend every night gorging at great restaurants, appetizer, entrée, and dessert twinned to superb beer. That's not my dining MO. Most nights, I eat dinner at home with my wife and daughter, plus or minus several friends. My Brooklyn kitchen is my preferred staging ground for pairings, mostly modest and low key in nature.

"Having five courses in three hours is a beautiful indulgence and, done well, it's a delightful evening," says Fred Bueltmann, author of *Beervangelist's Guide to the Galaxy: A Philosophy of Food and Drink*. "It's not how any of us are going to eat and drink seven days a week, and it's not how some people are going to eat and drink *any* days of the week."

Bueltmann is a self-professed explorer, storyteller, and former vice president of brand and lifestyle for Michigan's New Holland Brewing. In the last role,

Don't sweat it: beer pairings can be breezy and informal.

pull out some sausage, tomatoes, and cheese, paired with the pasta hiding in your pantry. Dinner is served. Pairings can be equally happy-go-lucky. "It could be, 'Of these three beers I have in my fridge, which one is going to go best with my steak dinner?'" Bueltmann says. "In life, we end up with more multiple-choice questions. It's not, 'If you could have any beer in the world within a four-hour drive, what would you have for dinner?' That's not how most people drink. Pairing needs to be rewarding and easy, not complicated and risky."

Fred Bueltmann, formerly of New Holland Brewing, recommends a simple approach to pairing beer with food.

★ ★ ★

Advice: "If I want to see how the food affects my perception of the beer, then I really need to have a bite of the food prior to my perception being altered by the beer. There's my control, then I'm going to go back to the beer."

—Fred Bueltmann, author, *Beervangelist's Guide to the Galaxy: A Philosophy of Food and Drink*

★ ★ ★

the epicurean orchestrated countless events and dinners, aiming to enlighten—sour beer is food's friend!—and make pairings more relatable and approachable, especially on the home front.

Have you opened your fridge on a sluggish Saturday night and wondered, What am I going to eat? Then you

WHY PAIR? BECAUSE YOU CARE

Dinner. Party. Those two words can pack hosts with equal parts excitement and anxiety, anticipation and dread. Screw societal expectations. You're not running a restaurant out of your kitchen. In my opinion, inviting friends and family over for dinner should be casual and carefree, low-fuss food paired with a couple of carefully chosen beers. It's an easy recipe for an excellent evening.

"If you're pairing in your home, you're showing people you've taken time, thought, love, care, and passion into what it is you're putting on the table," says British beer and food expert Melissa Cole, author of *The Beer Kitchen*.

Can't fire up a stove to save your life? That's fantastic. "You don't have to cook dinner to create an experience for your friends by thoughtfully combining beer and food," Bueltmann says. Think of nutty cheddar cheese served with a brown ale, or a raspberry lambic and some really good chocolate. Pairings are a gift of thoughtfulness. "It's saying, 'I've chosen what we're going to eat and drink based on how they relate to one another, and I'm offering it you, my guest.'"

For me, adding beer to eating is really about creating easy-glide pathways for conversation and connection. I rarely bare my soul over a Styrofoam plate and a glass of tepid tap water. Pair grilled sausages with pals and several six-packs of Anchor Steam, the char playing nice with the caramel richness? Now we're talking, and talking, and talking.

"Beer is a social lubricant that helps us all rub along a little bit better, and food is the social glue that sticks us all together for a little while. They stave off reality for a bit, and the big, bad outside world," Cole says. "You can bring those two things together in such a wonderful harmony. Why wouldn't you want that experience? If you love beer and you love food, why wouldn't you put in the tiniest bit of thought and the tiniest bit of legwork?"

British beer and food expert Melissa Cole, author of *The Beer Kitchen*.

Advice: Do dessert first, then finish with cheese. "Lingering over cheese boards with brandy balloon snifters filled with strong beer is an extremely civilized way to finish an evening," says *The Beer Kitchen* author Melissa Cole. Trying cheeses with different beers is a great way to stoke conversation without resorting to archetypal party talk about jobs, homes, school, and blah, blah, blah. "You're connecting on a very immediate and now level," she says. "It takes you out of your tribes and reminds people that they have more in common than what separates us. Particularly now, that's a really important thing."

BREWED AWAKENING: "Back in the early '80s, my stepdad gave me a bottle of Anchor Steam. It was just so different. The color was dark amber and the flavor just hit me on the palate. It was that 100 percent malt flavor with a bit of bitterness. I thought, I need to dig into this and figure out what makes this beer different."

—John Maier, brewmaster, Rogue Ales

STOP AND SMELL THE BEER

Slowing down and thinking is difficult in an always-on world spinning faster than an Olympic figure skater. Today, we eat fast food while driving really fast, and delivery drivers bring us piping-hot pizza in thirty minutes or less. Still, there's value in easing off the accelerator before packing your pie hole.

"If you don't stop to smell the beer, what's the point?" Cole says. She advises taking a wee bit of time to assess a beer's intensity, mouthfeel, and finish. "They're all easily recognizable things and signal flavor intensities," she says. Paralleling levels of strength is a great starting point for pairings. "In the same way that you don't take a sledgehammer to crack a walnut, you don't take a massive imperial stout and put it next to a prawn," she says. "You have no parity of power."

To instill pairing confidence, Bueltmann likes to ask for people's opinions on peanut butter and jelly sandwiches. Responses range from love to hate to that limbo emotion lost in the middle, *meh.* "You've been pairing since you were four years old and formed an opinion on two flavors brought together as part of a composition," he says. "That silly example is a reminder that you have this muscle and you've been exercising it for a long time. You know whether you want cream in your coffee. You know whether you want sugar on your grapefruit. You already have opinions. Everybody already has skills. Some people just haven't given themselves permission to apply that to beer and food."

The only thing better than beer? Beer *and* oysters.

He also encourages people not to nitpick over pairing beer with every edible on a plate. Think about flavor first and seek out bridges that will guide the rest of the meal. "We can create remarkable experiences in that fine-dining setting, but we can also mindfully select a beer for our main-and-two-sides dinner on a Tuesday night at home," Bueltmann says. Envision a coffee-rubbed grilled steak, creamy mashed potatoes, and broccoli finished with lemon and black pepper. "I could go with a roasty stout to accompany the steak,

★ ★ ★

Advice: Approach pairings from a culinary point of view. "If you look at the side of a bottle and it says, for example, it uses citrus peel and coriander seed and you know this style of beer is quite light, straight away citrus peel and coriander seed are things we know are used with fish dishes."

—Melissa Cole, author, *The Beer Kitchen*

★ ★ ★

FIVE TIPS FOR THROWING A BETTER BEER DINNER

★ ★ ★

1. **Course correction.** Less is more when it comes to the number of dishes. "I feel like four courses is the sweet spot," says Chris Davison, the head brewer at the food-focused Wolf's Ridge Brewing, in Columbus, Ohio. "I've done a lot of beer dinners that are five courses, and by the third or fourth course I am feeling pretty full. It's hard to enjoy the rest of it if you feel it's a chore to enjoy the food or beer. When you do a lot of courses, people often stop drinking beer or don't finish it."

2. **Size matters.** "People get way overexcited with portion sizes. If you want to do a genuine tasting menu, you've really got to keep it small," says *The Beer Kitchen* author Melissa Cole. "Portions shouldn't be much bigger than a very generous canapé, if you're going to go to seven, ten or fifteen courses. Tasting menus aren't supposed to leave you literally rolling out the door."

3. **Don't go big.** "There is an under-appreciation for starting subtle and elegant and ramping up from there," says Cole, who often starts classically with seafood and canapés and moves through a seafood course. "People have a tendency to want to try to wow straight out of the gate. There's no need to do that. If you start at a certain level, there's only one way to go. By the time you get to the cheese course, you're not only fat, you're also quite drunk."

4. **Pour move.** "It's important to not over-serve people," Davison says. "I've been to some beer dinners where they've served a full pint with every course. That's a lot of beer to give somebody."

5. **Bubble up.** Take carbonation into account. "It fills extra spaces that are normally reserved for food and flatter beverages," Cole says.

Chris Davison, head brewer at Wolf's Ridge Brewing.

or a nice assertive saison that might pick up the citrus and pepper out of the broccoli," Bueltmann says. "You have choices. It's saying, Pick one and see what you think. It's that moment of thoughtfulness and mindfulness."

★ ★ ★

Fun Fact: In 1998, I spent my college summer break abroad, living in London and working at the Great American Bagel Factory—no joke. I valiantly tried to get British customers to believe in the power of peanut butter and jelly. Customers were aghast at the combo, instead requesting butter and spreadable Marmite, a paste partly made from yeast extract. Lesson learned: changing hardwired opinions takes time.

★ ★ ★

NEW FLAVORS, NEW PAIRINGS

The luckiest books flame bright before fading from view, bottle rockets crashing back to earth. *The Brewmaster's Table* has broken popular culture's law of gravity. Brooklyn Brewery brewmaster Garrett Oliver published his influential and essential pairing work in 2003, an eternity ago in publishing, but the book is selling more copies now than it ever did, Oliver says. Notwithstanding the industry's tectonic changes, much about the brewing bedrock remains unchanged.

"What is fascinating from a beer point of view is that I've been around long enough that I've seen the hemlines move up and down, if you like, and the ties getting skinnier and wider over time," he says. "In beer, there aren't any specific new things. The only new things are flavors being derived from new hop varieties that would've been derived from somewhere else. It's all the same flavors. It's just a matter of the form they come in."

Beer flavors used to fit into rigidly defined boxes, pairings prearranged according to historical precedent. Citrus-bright witbiers went wonderfully with steamed mussels, sweet and burly barley wines stood toe to toe with blue cheese, elegantly fruity kölsch excelled with salad. By remixing and reconceptualizing, brewers have created new templates and possibilities for unions of food and beer.

"There are pairings that are going to be easier to do now than they would've been in the past because there might not be any new flavors, but there are new combinations and balances," Oliver says. Take the hazy New England IPA, especially one heaped with lactose, the unfermentable milk sugar that conveys sweetness. It's a peculiar permutation that may rankle purists who prefer IPAs drier than deadpan wit, but that sweet heresy cracks the code on a crazy-successful new combination. "If you have, say, really, really spicy Thai food, it's hard to find anything that pairs up better than one of those beers," Oliver says. "A double IPA that's really tropical with a little bit of sweetness from the lactose turns out to be perfect."

Brooklyn Brewery brewmaster Garrett Oliver.

Oliver was scheduled to host in Norway. One bottle was K Is for Kriek, a strong dark ale infused with dried Montmorency cherries, fermented with champagne and wild yeast, and aged in bourbon barrels. The pairing: local salmon.

"I'm sitting there thinking to myself, 'Cherries and salmon, that sounds really, really nasty.' I couldn't get my head around the pairing, but I went with it," Oliver says. "When the time came, the pairing was spectacular. The thing that I failed to recognize, despite all my experience, is that the

★ ★ ★

Advice: Why do so many fine-dining restaurants have drink menus bulging with pages of wine but only a few beers? Follow the money. Markups on wine can regularly run 300 to 400 percent. "Wine is the financial tent pole of a great many American restaurants," Garrett Oliver says. Adds Melissa Cole, "The biggest problem that beer has is that everybody knows the price of beer and the value of wine. The mystery of the wine industry and the mystery of restaurant pricing and the way that this is all worked out arbitrarily in closed rooms means that very few people realize that what they're drinking in restaurants has been marked up."

★ ★ ★

Now consider China's Sichuan cuisine, noted for its numbing, tingly, and fiery verve. "Maybe five, six, seven years ago I would've said, 'Oh, it has to be a saison,'" Oliver says. The farmhouse ale's classic lemony, peppery profile plays well with the Sichuan peppercorns' citrusy pop, while the high fizz helps douse heat. "Now you might have this range of very fruity IPAs that would work just as well."

For Oliver, all these new flavors are leading to new ways of thinking about pairings. Not too long ago, Brooklyn Brewery sent respected chef Roar Hildonen a selection of beers for a brewmaster's dinner that flavor of cherry is not the thing that matters. You're noticing it, sure, but when you're having a wine with salmon, you don't say, 'grapes and salmon.' The beer doesn't taste specifically like cherries. It tastes like itself."

Of late, Oliver has learned to shy away from linear thinking in terms of pairing. During one Hong Kong dinner, he matched lobster risotto with Black Ops, the bourbon barrel–aged imperial stout. "Rather than going for the obvious thing, I actually served it with a lobster risotto. My thinking was, lobster is fairly often served in a classical vanilla sauce. I have seen lobster risottos that had vanilla in them. In my head, despite it seeming so weird to do a barrel-aged imperial stout and a lobster risotto, I understood in my head that it should work. I told everybody, I might be running the car into a ditch here, but I think it's going to work. And it did work."

An eclectic selection from Burial Beer Co.'s kitchen in Asheville, North Carolina.

ONE IS THE MAGIC NUMBER: IN PRAISE OF THE ALL-PURPOSE BEER

★ ★ ★

As dad to a tornado of a daughter, I have little time for life's finer moments like, say, showering. Each day is a mad dash from morning to school to bedtime stories, after which I grab my reward: dinner and a beer, not always in that order.

I've often wondered whether there were a single do-it-all beer at ease with quesadillas, pad thai, roasted chicken, and takeout pizza alike, with enough character to keep me cranking through a six-pack. Would a dry, spicy, and brisk-sipping saison work?

"It's dangerous to recommend it as a one-size-fits-all style," says advanced Cicerone Mike Reis, now the co-owner of Redfield Cider Bar and Bottle Shop in Oakland, California. He cites the farmhouse ale's stylistic divergences, spanning from low-alcohol thirst-quenchers to *Brettanomyces*-spiked funk bombs.

"There are elements of intensity that can overpower more subtle dishes," Reis says. Instead, he suggests malt-forward German Märzens or Vienna lagers. "These beers are moderate in strength, so you're not going to risk overpowering more delicate

flavors earlier on in the meal." While he notes their affinity for sausages, roast pork, and duck, "you're not going to encounter as many blow-your-mind pairings," Reis says. On the flip side, "you're much less likely to have clashing flavors."

Food and beer guru Fred Bueltmann echoes Reis's suggestion. "I find malt-forward beers with slight caramel notes to be ultimately versatile," says Bueltmann, name-checking brown ales and bocks. "They evoke the flavor brought from the Maillard reaction* so common in cooking and foods." That means a fondness for bacon, crusty pretzels, browned onions, seared steak and scallops, and baked bread—even you, pizza.

What about my old pal IPA? No go, says Master Cicerone Mirella Amato. With pairings, "the two things to watch out for are hops and alcohol," she says. "When those elements are high, they can pose problems." For a jack-of-all-trades ale, Amato emphasizes cuisine's importance. She favors Italian food, which excels with the understated complexity of English-style pale ales and bitters. "The herbal notes from the hops mirror the kind of herbs I use, such as basil and oregano."

The next time I baked pasta with tomato sauce—a go-to for my wife and daughter—Firestone Walker's DBA was sublime. When I smashed burgers in a cast-iron pan, Paulaner's Oktoberfest-Märzen was pitch-perfect. Those two beers immediately found a permanent fridge perch, at the ready to elevate everyday dinner. While there's still a place in my life for a multicourse meal paired with many beers, I've come to appreciate the potent power of one.

*The Maillard reaction, a.k.a. "browning," is a set of chemical reactions that occur when amino acids and reducing sugars are introduced to heat.

BREWED AWAKENING:

"Back in 2013, while thinking about new beers to brew, I envisioned a beer that smelled like a Saturday morning breakfast, the aroma of freshly brewed coffee and that sweet smell of pancakes and maple syrup. My first batch was pretty good—the coffee was present, but the maple character was missing. The tricky thing about brewing with maple syrup is that it's fermentable, so yeast gobble sugars and flavor. So I brewed it over and over, experimenting with every possible maple product: light maple syrup, dark maple syrup, dehydrated maple syrup, maple sugar, various extracts, and even maple butter. My wife kept asking when our house would stop smelling like maple! Eventually,

I discovered a highly distilled Vermont maple syrup product and figured out a unique process to lock in the flavor for what became Double Stack, our imperial breakfast stout."

—James Dugan, cofounder and co-brewer, Great Notion Brewing

BREWERIES ELEVATE THE RESTAURANT GAME

Brewpubs were once the main pathway for buying from-the-source beer. You'd sit at the bar, order a dozen chicken wings or maybe a burger and fries, then drink a couple of pints. Now, breweries are deep-sixing the deep fryer and opening kitchen-free taprooms, outsourcing sustenance to food trucks and pop-up vendors.

For beer fans, this has become a fork in the road: "More and more beer lovers are going to tasting-room

A selection of East Coast oysters on offer at Dogfish Head's Chesapeake & Maine restaurant.

breweries for the beer experience and, secondarily, there may be food trucks there to fill their stomachs," says Dogfish Head's Calagione. "It's not the driver of that visit. When they're thinking more about, 'Oh, I want an amazing food and beer experience,' that's when they're seeking out higher-end restaurants. . . . One is more about the beer and food is secondary. One is more about the food and beer is secondary, but they love both."

In response, breweries have upped their gastronomic game, building ingredient-obsessed restaurants right in line with our contemporary dining moment. Along the same line as beer, food has been elevated from fuel to flavorful art form, a mass-market commodity gone local. It's no longer enough to serve frozen Sysco chicken fingers alongside that unfiltered lager filled with corn grown by that farmer down the road.

Dogfish Head's Chesapeake & Maine is a nautically inspired seafood restaurant that sources its mussels, crabs, lobsters, and more from its namesake regions, nodding to the brewery's location in the Chesapeake Bay and Maine, where Calagione spent summers. "We're maniacally committed to freshness with beer, so let's show an equal level of maniacal commitment to freshness in seafood," he says, noting that most seafood sold in American restaurants arrives frozen and from distant waters.

Seattle's venerable Pike Brewing now runs Tankard and Tun, celebrating the Pacific Northwest's natural pantry in dishes such as albacore loin ceviche and pulled-mushroom sandwiches topped with

Trillium Brewing operates a Boston restaurant offering New England–inspired farmhouse fare.

house-made ricotta. Burial Beer's Asheville, North Carolina kitchen serves locally produced charcuterie, such as Lady Edison Extra Fancy Country Ham. In Boston, Trillium Brewing Company operates a three-story restaurant serving "New England farmhouse inspired food" such as wood-fired root vegetables and foie gras paired with granola made from spent brewing grain.

These fresh approaches aren't just about menus. The dining experiences emphasize relaxation and

a lazier pace, breathing space for contemplating more than just another order of onion rings. "The service is intentionally a little deeper and slower," Calagione says.

The Brewpub Menu Moves beyond Mozzarella Sticks

Making a brewpub menu once required little more than a low-wattage light-bulb moment. Throw some mozzarella sticks on there, add burgers and nachos, give kids chicken fingers or grilled cheese, and—look at that!—lunch, dinner, and brunch were served. Dining at brewpubs once felt like the culinary equivalent of *Groundhog Day*, where you ate the same thing over and over. Now, brewpubs are becoming fine-dining destinations, creating idiosyncratic synergies of food and beer.

In Austin, Texas, the Brewer's Table turns out smoked rabbit carnitas in pig blood–infused mole, bouillabaisse swimming with hop-cured scallops, and venison tartare finished with toasted brewer's yeast, carefully coupled with wood-aged lagers. Atlanta's

Wrecking Bar Brew Pub follows a strict farm-to-table script, going so far as to operate its own sixty-two-acre farm that supplies produce and fowl for dishes such as the chicken-and-liver sausage and beef-heart tartare.

The brewpub Edmund's Oast, in Charleston, South Carolina, opened in 2014 with a fully articulated vision of being a great restaurant that could stand on its kitchen's bona fides, irrespective of the beer. "We specifically wanted to avoid the bratwursts, cheese dips, pretzels, and schnitzels that might typically grace the menu at a brewpub," says Advanced Cicerone Brandon Plyler, the beer buyer and educator at Edmund's Oast. "I love dipping schnitzel into cheese dip with a mustard-covered brat chaser, but giving the chef the freedom to develop their menu the way they want, without compromise, is a great way to start."

Today, the warmly inviting restaurant, where old cutting boards double as wall art and chandeliers are suspended from the cypress wood ceiling, serves the likes of red curry eggplant, chicken liver parfait, and fried tripe finished with a Korean-inspired vinaigrette. They're paired with more than forty draft beers, including house creations such as the Lord Proprietor's Mild, which is steeped with locally grown black tea, and the Sour Bradford Watermelon, which stars the Southern heirloom fruit prized for its sweetness and perfumed red flesh. When guests sit at the chef's counter and order the seven-course tasting menu, the accompanying beverage pairings could start with a negroni, move to a sherry, then to a Belgian tripel, then to a glass of Gamay, and finish

The dining room scene at Edmund's Oast, a brewpub in Charleston, South Carolina.

with a barrel-aged beer. "We place beer on the same elevated level as the wine and cocktails," Plyler says. "Keeping all of these elements on an equal playing field helps with the picture that the beer is on par with everything else."

Brewery Bhavana, in Raleigh, North Carolina, is on par with *nothing* else. It's a bookstore, a newsstand, a flower shop, and a dim sum restaurant serving soup dumplings and steamed buns stuffed with Cantonese-style barbecue pork, largely paired with Belgian-inspired beer. "As a brewer, I've always been attracted to the complex aromatics of Belgian beers and the ease with which you can pair them with many different cuisines," says brewer and cofounder Patrick Woodson. "Dim sum and Cantonese cuisine tend to focus on subtle flavors that are more nuanced than bold. We strive to brew beer in the same vein, so that no single flavor outshines the overall experience."

The food menu rarely stays static for long, giving Woodson ample opportunity to explore new flavor arrangements, such as aging a Belgian-style dubbel on dried figs. "It pairs effortlessly with more decadent

Presentation is increasingly important as brewery restaurants take their culinary game to the next level.

dishes like Peking duck," he says. "The crispy skin and hoisin sauce really play against the roundness of the beer, with its sweet aromatics and crisp, dry finish." The savory elements of spicy and anesthetizing pork belly rice cakes inspired him to create the Norwegian Farmhouse Sour, featuring pink peppercorns, grapefruit zest, and kveik yeast. (See page 177 for more on the Scandinavian yeast.) "It's a bright and tropical contrast to the heat and fat of that dish but with

super-high carbonation that simultaneously refreshes the palate and accentuates the Sichuan peppercorn's numbing sensation," he says.

★ ★ ★

Fun Fact: An oast house is a building designed for drying hops.

★ ★ ★

BATTER UP: THE SCIENCE BEHIND BEER-BATTERED FOOD

★ ★ ★

Next time you crunch into some shatteringly crisp fish and chips, chances are you should thank your good buddy beer. It's essential to the best batters, contributing a trifecta of crucial ingredients: alcohol, foaming agents, and carbon dioxide. Bubbles expand when batter hits hot oil, creating the delicately crunchy texture, W. Wayt Gibbs and Nathan Myhrvold, the lead author of *Modernist Cuisine*, explain in *Scientific American*. Beer works so well because the bubbles are encased in a protective thin film that pumps the brakes on bursting. Also, because alcohol evaporates faster than water, the batter quickly crunches up, minimizing the risk of overcooking food.

Beer is key to the crunchiest batter.

YES, CHEF: HOW THE KITCHEN CAN INFLUENCE BEER

Chefs and brewers didn't always work closely together, the stove and brew kettle separate fiefdoms of flavor. But increasingly, brewers and cooks are working closer than ever, a win-win for taste buds everywhere.

Wolf's Ridge Brewing is one of the finer restaurants in Columbus, Ohio, the sort of place you'd go on a promising third date and splurge on, say, the paprika foam-topped sea scallops served with fried bread and citrus egg-yolk jam. The beers, too, find creative culinary footing, including Daybreak, a brunch-worthy cream ale lightly flavored with coffee and vanilla beans.

One day, head brewer Chris Davison was trying to figure out how to incorporate fennel into beer and was considering cold-steeping fennel seeds. Instead, the kitchen crew recommended using some of the fresh

Scallops topped with caviar are paired with a saison at Wolf's Ridge Brewing in Columbus, Ohio.

fennel root earmarked for salad. "You can get the same flavor without the bitterness that seeds would've imparted," he recalls. In the end, the kitchen cooked down the fennel root on the stove with some beer, and added it to another lager alongside lavender or sage. "It tastes just like breakfast sausage," Davison says of the beer, called Link or Patty? "I never would've thought to make the beer that way if it weren't for the chefs. They're teaching me to look at ingredients in a different way, from a processing standpoint."

Chicago's Band of Bohemia might be the most successful intersection of brewing and cooking. It opened in 2015 and, within a year, had earned its first Michelin star, one of fine dining's most distinguished awards and the first bestowed to a brewpub. It steamrolls clichés left and right, the room decorated like an old parlor with plush couches, curved paisley booths, and elephant-print curtains, a record player spinning tunes from yesteryear.

Behind the bar, there's a glass wall that provides a peek into the brewhouse where cofounder and head brewer Michael Carroll makes his crisply delicate Jasmine Rice lager and Indian Pale Ale (yes, that *n* should be there) flavored with spices including cardamom, cloves, and kaffir lime leaves. It's beer that *wants* to go with food, underscored by Band of Bohemia's reverse approach to pairing: the beer recipe comes first, then the dish is designed. "From a chef standpoint, you have to think about things that you normally wouldn't think about," Carroll says. "It makes you think outside the box a little bit."

Mull over the changing seasons: A chef might come in with a ready-made list of seasonal ingredients and potential combinations. "With the reverse part of it, you have to taste the beer and pull it apart," Carroll says. Say the chef wanted to serve an in-season pickled vegetable such as fall carrots or radishes. But do they work with the beer? Are they too sour? Should they be sweeter? What's missing?

Above all, the goal isn't to echo similarities but to have the beer and dish fill in the blanks. "If you taste the beer and get banana spice and clove, then you pair that with, like, banana with a clove caramel, you're just making the same thing," Carroll says. "It's like ordering a steak with a steak. It's not adding the same thing. It's adding what you're missing. . . . We try to complement each other by having the differences come together as one."

The approach has been critically validated year after year, with Band of Bohemia acquiring its third straight Michelin star in 2018. That puts the brewpub in a pretty funny position. Despite the fact that "culinary brewhouse" is written on the side of the brick building, many customers are attracted, moth to light, by the promise of Michelin star–validated food. "There are plenty of people that still don't know we're a brewery, which is amusing to me," Carroll says.

Charred octopus at Band of Bohemia, Chicago's Michelin-starred brewpub.

"They can sit at the bar for 20 minutes and talk to the bartender and be like, 'What is this place?' 'It's a brewery.' 'Where's the brewery?' 'You've been staring at it. It's right behind the glass wall.'"

★ ★ ★

Advice: "My No. 1 rule, personally, is that I tend to hate beer with dessert. Everyone wants to pair beer with dessert. When you pair something sweet with almost any type of beer, it tends to accentuate the bitterness of that beer. However, lighter or fruity beers with a sorbet can be amazing."

—Chris Davison, head brewer, Wolf's Ridge Brewing

★ ★ ★

With Brewed Food, Denver chef Jensen Cummings applies brewing techniques and ingredients to cooking.

JENSEN CUMMINGS

Founder, Brewed Food

★ ★ ★

Jensen Cummings favors a different set of ingredients from most chefs. He ferments yogurt with brewing yeast, adds crystal malt to sauerkraut, creates hop vinegar, and makes beef jerky with malt extract. It's both a scientific and gastronomic endeavor to connect cooking and brewing, a concept and company that he calls Brewed Food.

"Our lens is looking at brewing techniques and ingredients as culinary ingredients," Cummings says. "Yeast is the center of that conversation. We want to say that yeast is a culinary ingredient."

Since founding Brewed Food in 2014, he has worked with a revolving cast of brewing collaborators, such as New Belgium and Jester King, and chefs to rewire beer's relationship to all things edible. The experimental ground zero is Cummings's Denver test kitchen, where a large white-board is filled with fermentation fantasies, such as turning classic pairings like strawberries with black pepper into beer. "We'll do a beer aged on strawberries with no black pepper. We want to coax out those pepper notes with a mixed culture or maybe some saison yeast," he says.

Cummings and company will take any sugar source (honey, agave syrup, etc.) and ferment it with upward of fifty yeast strains to see which functions best. This technical work, done in conjunction with local yeast lab Inland Island, is Brewed Food's biggest undertaking. There are books aplenty on brewing with yeast, but, as he explains, "We're fermenting solid mediums, not liquid."

He quickly learned the specific challenges during early attempts to convert cabbage into kimchi. "The plant matter just disintegrated," Cummings says. "It tasted great, if you want a bowl of gruel. Many of our fermentations were epic failures of not understanding that sugar isn't sugar and what fermentation activity would do to plant matter."

Cummings's fix is multiphase fermentation. The first couple of weeks, while souring *Lactobacillus* bacteria does the heavy lifting, Cummings ferments yeast in sugar water. "We call that our MSG. It's pure flavor," he says. He then pours the mixture onto kimchi and adds additional yeast. "It's like mounting a sauce with butter."

(continued on next page)

The "Crooked Stave pork" from Brewed Food in Denver, Colorado.

The chef wasn't always so crazy about beer, once crushing "dirty thirties" of Milwaukee's Best. Cooking, though, is coded into his DNA. His family has been in the restaurant business for five generations. In Little Falls, Minnesota, his great-great grandfather ran La Fond House ("It looked like someplace where Wyatt Earp shot somebody out front, a straight-up corner saloon," he says), and his great-grandfather and grandfather operated restaurants and bars in San Francisco. While Cummings's dad "can't boil an egg," his father's three younger brothers own restaurants in Ames, Iowa.

After barely graduating high school in San Diego, Cummings learned the kitchen ropes at his uncle's Ames sports bar and, in time, attended the Iowa Culinary Institute. His beverage teacher doubled as a general manager for the local Rock Bottom Restaurant and Brewery, which the students toured. "I had no concept there was a human being creating something with their hands," he says of meeting the brewer.

He began educating his palate on global beers, falling in love with both New Belgium Fat Tire and his now-wife, Betsy. While Betsy finished college, Cummings moved to Kansas City to work at the influential 40 Sardines (since shuttered). At a Boulevard Brewing beer dinner, he sampled an early version of Tank 7, a dry and fruity exultation of farmhouse perfection. "I was like, 'This is what it needs to be about,' creating something new, something interesting, something exciting that I'd never seen," he says.

Brewery-drenched Denver was the couple's next move. There, Cummings secured his Cicerone certification, worked as a restaurant group's beer buyer, and brewed collaborative beers with Bull and Bush, "trying

Grains are often prepared in a miso broth.

any way I could to scratch and claw into a position where I could have a serious conversation about beer and food."

He sought the connections between brewing and cooking, discovering a link: spent grain. That waste product could be repurposed as food, a bond between cooks of a different kind. Cummings's insight sits at the core of Brewed Food. "The brewer is a chef and the brew house is a kitchen," he says. In addition to raising two young sons, he takes Brewed Food on the road to restaurants and breweries such as Cincinnati's Rhinegeist and Seattle's Fremont and has a line of packaged goods, including soy sauce and kimchi. Under the Good Bugs mantle, he's created collaborative beers with more than twenty breweries, including Crooked Stave, Trve, and Blackberry Farm.

Fermentation's serial thrills fuel Cummings's trials as he forges new pathways for integrating beer and cuisine. "Brewed Food was built on the belief that beer and food—and, more importantly, brewing and cooking—can and should be the pinnacle of culinary experience," he says. "That's the sentence I look at and say, 'Am I doing everything that I can to drive that home?'"

TAKE A SEAT WITH THE TABLE (BEER)

I have fond, if foggy, memories of college dinner parties fueled by four-liter jugs of Carlo Rossi wine. The bottle's chief virtues were its low price, large volume of inoffensive liquid, and ability to sit sentry next to the butter, napkins, and bread. We never discussed Carlo. Table wine, as the loose category of affordable mealtime accompaniments is called, facilitated dialogue without serving as a focal point.

These days, you won't find table wine accompanying my dinner spread. Instead, I favor table *beer*, an agreeable and unpretentious accompaniment to good food and good times. Table beer is generally not aggressively hopped or intensely flavored. It's simply beer for drinking, perfect whether you're eating pizza, salad, oysters, or grocery-store rotisserie chicken. "This is a beer to put on the table with friends, family, and food, and to complement that idyllic scenario," says Blake Tyers, the wood cellar

Food-friendly table beers pair well with a wide range of cuisines.

FOUR FAIL-SAFE BEER PAIRINGS

★ ★ ★

Meat Your Match: Burgers and steaks go gangbusters with a roasty yet light-drinking dark lager like Köstritzer Schwarzbier or a porter like Deschutes Black Butte, which will find a charred accord.

Totally Tubular: A gently floral, refined kölsch—Germany's legendary Gaffel Kölsch and Reissdorf Kölsch are great—excels with salads and lighter sausages like bratwurst.

Shell Game: The citrusy tartness of a spritzy Berliner weisse like Evil Twin Nomader Weisse or Fierce, from Off Color, is a killer brunch counterpoint to eggs, especially Benedict or Florentine, as well as oysters.

Slice Is Nice: Amber lagers' lingering sweetness tempers tomato sauce's acidic sting, while brisk carbonation and moderate bitterness chop through pizza's rich cheese. Try Great Lakes Eliot Ness or Devils Backbone Vienna Lager.

and specialty brand manager for Creature Comforts Brewing.

Table beer dates to nineteenth-century Belgium, where tafelbier (Flemish for "table beer"), the light-bodied, low-alcohol ale—usually less than 3 percent ABV—often accompanied mealtime for adults and kids alike. (Belgian schoolchildren drank versions deep into the twentieth century.) In Belgium, table beers slid from relevancy, losing ground to soft drinks and bottled water, but American brewers have embraced the food-friendly beer's flavorful potential.

Table beer is more of a malleable concept than a rigid construct, an idea open to infinite interpretation. Allagash's coriander-spiced River Trip and Kent Falls' Farmer's Table favor IPA-worthy aromas. Jester King's Le Petit Prince is rustic and effervescent, while Central State's lightly funky Table is fermented with wild yeast. In Brooklyn, I regularly drink Threes Brewing's clean and lightly lemony Table Beer, maybe with a pickle-topped cheeseburger.

"Generally we believe there should be a beer designed for drinking and eating," Tyers says. "The intent of the beer is to live on the table with food and if it matches that, the beer can certainly be in a table beer category." Creature Comforts worked with chefs to create its plainly named Table Beer. It's a Belgian-style blonde with an earthy, floral fragrance; mild appetite-stoking bitterness; and palate-cleaning minerality. "It supports eating food without getting in the way too much," Tyers says.

NOODLING AROUND WITH RAMEN AND BEER

★ ★ ★

Ivan Ramen owner and chef Ivan Orkin with a selection of beers served at his NYC restaurants.

Growing up, one of my family's favorite lazy-Saturday meals was cheap instant ramen. "You just have to doctor it up," my dad would say, ripping open the plastic package with his teeth, brittle white noodles tumbling onto the kitchen counter.

While the salty broth burbled and the squiggly noodles softened, he added sesame oil, scallions, garlic, onions, and mushrooms, then swirled in a raw egg. Cost-effective sustenance became ambrosia, a tradition I continue to this day, albeit with one tweak: now I alternate slurps with sips

(continued on next page)

of beer, a pro move in my opinion and that of Cat Brackett, the general manager and beverage director at New York City's permanently mobbed Ivan Ramen, a hallowed ground for noodle heads and beer nerds alike.

"Beer and ramen make so much sense together," Brackett says. "They have so much in common." At its core, beer is composed of four ingredients (yeast, water, hops, and grain) that brewers spin in delicious directions. Ramen is also built from four basic building blocks, counting noodles, toppings, broth, and tare, the flavorings that include miso (fermented soybeans), *shio* (salt), and *shoyu* (soy sauce). From there, ramen is open

New York City's Ivan Ramen focuses on pairing beer with the Japanese noodle soup.

Ramen is not the only thing on offer at New York City's Ivan Ramen.

to interpretation, such as Ivan Ramen's decadent chicken paitan, which tastes as if an entire fowl were slowly simmered and condensed into a single bowl.

"Ramen is very expressive, and beer is very much that same way," Brackett says. To create pairing contrasts and flavorful convergences, Brackett has built a far-ranging, fast-changing beer menu that veers from Holy Mountain's Ox, an oak-aged farmhouse ale zapped with *Brettanomyces* and orange zest, to rarely seen Belgian lambics and hard-to-get IPAs from of-the-moment breweries

like Sweden's Brewski and The Answer, from Richmond, Virginia.

"There are so many fats in ramen, and beer works really well at cutting through the fat," she says, noting that soured beers are well suited to the task. Many customers come in ready for a flavor ride, served up by the bowl and pint, but timeless styles are worth revisiting as well. "We always try to keep a crisp pilsner or rice lager in stock," she says. (You'll regularly find Japan's refreshing Orion.) "Everyone can crush a pilsner while crushing bowls of ramen."

DRINKING DESTINATION

Brussels: Why You Should Visit Belgium's Beer-Culture City

Yvan De Baets, cofounder and brewmaster, Brasserie de la Senne

★ ★ ★

Brasserie de la Senne cofounder Yvan De Baets.

At the turn of the twentieth century, the Brussels region was one of the world's great brewing centers, having roughly 250 breweries and an equal number of lambic blenders. Their spontaneously fermented beers were the country's most sought after, and they exported their gueuze to the United States as early as the 1840s. (In 1881, Brussels even topped Munich for the world's highest beer consumption, with an annual 455 liters a head.)

By 2010, though, only one brewery remained in Brussels proper: Brasserie Cantillon. That year, we opened Brussels' first modern brewery, Brasserie de la Senne, to brew the beers we wanted to drink but couldn't find. We combined our love of European hops with the history of brewing in Belgium, as well as the United Kingdom and Germany, to create (noble) hop-forward beers and *Brettanomyces*-fermented beers. Some call our approach modern-traditionalist, or maybe traditional-modernist. We call it Brasserie de la Senne.

Nowadays, beer once more flows through the city like the Senne River, and five authentic breweries produce all their beer in Brussels. (I'm excluding contract brewers, locally called fake brewers.) But hey, it's the quality, not the quantity, right? Breweries in Brussels represent a rich diversity of styles, brewing methods, and approaches. Cantillon, where cobwebs hang from ceilings and barrels, is a lambic lover's mecca. En Stoemelings revisits good old Belgian classics (try Curieuse Neus, a tripel), and L'Ermitage Nanobrasserie makes US-oriented brews such as the fruity Lanterne pale ale. No Science combines English

Bottles of spontaneously fermented beer at Brasserie Cantillon in Brussels, Belgium.

The Grand Place is the scenic central square of Brussels.

and American tones in its porters and rye pale ales. And this is just the beginning of a new wave of breweries in Brussels.

Beyond breweries, what defines Brussels as a beer destination is how people can interact with our beer culture. It's not in a history book; it's in our cafés. Their beauty is they are cozy and unpretentious, in a way that will make you immediately feel at home, no matter your age, class, culture, or ethnicity. Everyone gathers easily over beer, provided they respect one unwritten rule: "Behave correctly and you will be warmly welcomed, whoever you are." We call this *zinneke*, the local word that best defines our city and lends it an extra soul. Though the word originally described a mutt, *zinneke* is now how we say that something is a mix of different origins, a rare treat not often seen around the world. (Our main beer, a hoppy and malty pale ale with a fine bitterness called Zinnebir, is a tribute to that idea.)

You'll discover plenty of that *zinneke* spirit at beer cafés in downtown Brussels. I love them because they're places where real people go, and the beer is guaranteed to be fresh. Le Coq is a perfect example of a café with a laid-back atmosphere.

Booze 'n' Blues is the Brussels equivalent of an American music bar, created by a guy who never visited the States but still got the right feel. It offers great beer and bourbon, but most of all it's a place with character. Poechenellekelder is located in front of the iconic Manneken Pis statue, that little peeing hero. Decorated with puppets, the quirky café should be a tourist trap, but locals like me go there to enjoy great Belgian beers and the warm, welcoming vibe. Dolle Mol is the second coming of a legendary literary and anarchistic bar. It's tamer now but retains the open-minded and offbeat spirit of the original, with its walls covered with tributes to "Belgitude"—what we call our cultural identity.

To find the most *zinneke* gastronomic restaurant, head to Les Brigittines, where chef Dirk Myny serves dishes like Cantillon kriek–braised veal and wild boar terrine, perhaps paired with a gueuze. He's the quintessential Brussels spirit—serious in work, crazy when it's time to party—with a typical sense of the local humor we call *zwanze*.

It's tough to describe, so you'll need to visit Brussels to experience it yourself.

BREWED AWAKENING: "When I was 15, my father (who is a doctor) took a one-year sabbatical in France, and my parents hauled my four sibs and me over for the year. We traveled all over France, Switzerland, Germany, Belgium, and we visited relatives in Ireland. That year in Europe opened my eyes to the culture of enjoying life through food and drink. I drank some beer then, but it wasn't until I went to college that I became the beer expert among my friends. I believe our travels to Europe really planted the seed for me."

—Brian Dunn, founder, Great Divide Brewing

A La Mort Subite is one of Brussels' classic bars.

TOASTING THE FUTURE

A ROAD MAP TO DELICIOUS NEW DIRECTIONS

t's peculiar to live life perched at the crossroads of the past and the future, the analog and the digital. I was born in 1978, and as a kid, I rushed outside to grab the *Dayton Daily News*, our local Ohio newspaper, to see whether the Cincinnati Reds won last night's baseball game. I shopped for clothes at the mall and connected with friends over a phone call. I cut and pasted (with scissors!) images and angst-ridden teenage tales to create my high school zine, *Taste Our Love*, running off copies at the local Staples—and then running out the door without paying, a different generation's approach to pirating.

But I'm no Luddite calling for the return of VCRs and paying by check at the supermarket. Modern times have brought us the marvels of instant messaging and instant news, online shopping for when I'm too lazy to put on a pair of jeans to buy some new ones. Maybe our near future will welcome drone-based delivery,

155

Pouring a beer sample into a lab beaker.

whirling wingamathings wordlessly bringing us hot pepperoni pizza, crispy General Tso's chicken, and cold beer. But what kind of beer? That's the inquiry that keeps me (mostly) gainfully employed as a journalist.

In my earlier days with beer, there were distinct pathways that consumers would follow to gain access to Beer Knowledge™. That meant trying monk-made dubbels and tripels, along with some Saison Dupont, Orval, and, if lucky, Westvleteren 12. The strong and brooding Trappist ale, redolent of dark fruit, was once regarded as the world's best, worthy of a bucket-list trip to the Belgian monastery where the beer is made and mainly sold. At a Massachusetts beer festival called, appropriately, the Festival, I once drank Westy 12 and felt as if I'd summited the Mount Everest of beer nerddom. Look at me, mom! I'm a real beer drinker now!

That achievement now feels as dated as the tape player in our 2003 Subaru. Beer's time-honored entry points and benchmarks have been disrupted as thoroughly as tech companies disrupted print by taking aim at the dead-tree media. Who cares about tradition when you have glittery IPAs, stouts reminiscent of breakfast pastries, and pungent pale ales that taste like a rip from a vape pen?

And that's just fine! When it comes to writing recipes, everything and anything is fair game for breweries today. Beer is a dynamic beverage capable of taking on new forms to captivate taste buds. That makes it pretty tough to predict the future. Who knows what fads will percolate through the cultural pipeline in a year's time? I mean, I never would've guessed that brewers would add activated charcoal to beer, making pints that look a bit like liquid steel wool.

Nonetheless, the hoppy winds are blowing in a couple of distinct directions. Breweries will continue to refine their approach to wild and sour beers, as well as create new crossovers between beer and wine. Nonalcoholic beers will finally gain that missing component—flavor—as breweries seek to satisfy consumers who crave a couple of cold ones, minus the buzz. Instead, perhaps you'll order an alcohol-free beer infused with THC, marijuana's psychoactive

BREWED AWAKENING: "My beer epiphany took place soon after college. The beer was Belgium's Tripel Karmeliet, served on tap, which is still a rarity in the US as far as I can tell. The first sip grabbed my attention in a visceral and startling way: the room grew quiet, my vision focused on the glass in my hand, and my brain struggled to make sense of the incredible liquid I'd just consumed. The flavor was shocking, and I enjoyed it immensely. From that sip on, I was hooked, and it eventually led me to start this sprawling, complicated company that now rules my life."

—Jacob McKean, CEO and founder, Modern Times Beer

compound, chased by a tropical IPA that derives its fruity notes from kveik, a kind of Norwegian farmhouse yeast. But really, some days don't you just want a perfectly refreshing pilsner?

After all, some beers never go out of style, no matter what's *in* style.

Yazoo Brewing's "Embrace the Funk" series of beers are made with an assortment of wild yeasts, souring microbes, and wooden casks.

A SOUR TASTE

I cannot say I enjoyed the first few times I drank sour beer. The flavor reminded me of drinking orange juice after brushing my teeth, or the insanely tart Warheads candies I popped during high school, more dare than delight. Joke's on me!

"Seven or eight years ago, people thought it was funny to hand people a bottle of New Belgium's La Folie"—a sour brown ale first produced in 1998—"and say, 'Try this,'" says brewer Brandon Jones, the blender at Nashville's Yazoo Brewing Company. "It is different than anything you've ever been told beer is," Jones says of sour and wild beer. "Visually and aromatically, it's just completely different."

Many early American sours followed an arc of intensity familiar to longtime IPA fans. "When the IPA movement started taking off in the mid-2000s, think how bitter some beers got," says Jeffers Richardson, the director of Barrelworks, Firestone Walker's sour and wild facility. "Look where we are with IPAs now. It's a completely different market in terms of levels of bitterness, aromas, and alcohol levels. The sour and wild movement was pretty similar. Some of the early starters produced some really tart beers. Initially, everyone just went for the extremes of acidity."

That's no shock, given modern brewers' natural tendency to stretch styles like rubber bands. "When we get on something we try to push the envelope and see where the borders are," Richardson says. "That allows for a lot of good exploration, but eventually we might just overwhelm somebody's palate and we might just dial it back."

Jeffers Richardson is the director of Barrelworks, Firestone Walker's sour and wild facility.

Advice: "Just because your friends like a lot of acidity and you don't, that's OK. There's no shame in that. We don't have to chest bump because we can take the highest level of Scoville units or the highest IBUs or the highest level of acid."

—Jeffers Richardson, director, Firestone Walker Barrelworks

Don't Use *That* Word

As IPAs have grown more approachable, so have sour beers, a phrase I shouldn't really be using. "If anybody has heard me get up on my soapbox, the term 'sour' to describe a whole category of beer bugs me," Richardson says. "It assumes everything has to be really sour. People just say 'sour' without understanding there's not just one type of acidity."

To help consumers recognize acidity's role and contribution to beer, Richardson leads seminars called—wait for it—Jeffers Drops Acid . . . Knowledge.

His roving tutorials, which started in 2014, delve into acid's sensory impacts. "It's half geek class, half sensory," he says. "We can measure acid with our tongues in terms of tartness, but there's no way for us to talk about your level of what you think is strong and my level. They may be two different things."

He starts demonstrations by giving attendees two samples, each containing a different acid: acetic (vinegary) and lactic (sharp and focused). "Those are acids that one is likely to see in a wild or sour beer," he says. Then he asks his students whether the samples are the same or different. "Everyone at the end yells, 'Different,'" he says. "It's a bit of a trick question because it depends how you're measuring it."

★ ★ ★

Advice: "Beer is about drinkability. I think people taste at bottle shares, and they are drinking one, two, or three ounces of something. At that level, we can taste and finish whatever we're drinking. To me it's, 'Would you pour yourself a pint of this?' When you have high levels of acetic acid, it doesn't sit well in your stomach. How much of that beer do you want to drink? You go to Belgium and see people drinking a few glasses of their local lambic. Why is that? Because it's not at a nuclear level of acidity."

—Jeffers Richardson, director, Firestone Walker Barrelworks

★ ★ ★

AN ACID EXPLAINER

Flunk organic chemistry? Me too! Here are four of the most common organic acids you'll encounter in beer.

★ ★ ★

Acetic: I have one word for you: vinegar. Good in small doses, off-putting in higher concentrations.

Citric: It supplies citrus fruits such as lemons, grapefruits, and limes with their signature tang.

Lactic: This acid delivers the soft, clean tartness that's familiar to fans of fermented foods such as yogurt and sour cream.

Malic: When you bite into a green apple, malic acid is responsible for that subdued, enticing, mouth-watering tartness.

Bonus fact: You'll find citric and malic acids, among others, in many popular puckering candies such as Sour Patch Kids, Warheads, and SweeTARTS.

The two main methods of measuring a beer's acidity are potential of hydrogen (pH) and titratable, or total, acidity (TA). "If you measure acidity with pH, they're exactly the same," Richardson says. The problem with pH is that it's a broad measure—yes, acidity exists. It is a thing. "But you taste a difference, and titratable acidity measures the difference." TA is a better measure of how acidic a beer tastes to *you*, underscoring Richardson's main point: not all acids taste identical (see box on page 160).

REMEMBER, TIME IS MONEY

Not every acerbic beer rides the same microbial road. Brewers utilize distinct blends of souring bacteria, chiefly *Lactobacillus* and *Pediococcus*, and sometimes the wild yeast *Brettanomyces*. These minute and marvelous creatures clock in and work about as fast as the folks s-l-o-w-l-y fixing the New York City subway system.

But the payoff arrives in flavor. Beer makers find it worthwhile to give bug-ridden beverages months or even years to convert sugars into a multifaceted range

Beer patiently slumbers in barrels while wild yeast and souring bacteria work away.

of tastes and fragrances, acidity served up alongside fruit, funk, and earth. When ready, these beers regularly cost fifteen or twenty dollars per wine-size bottle, a fee that consumers should pay with no questions asked. And yet questions will always be asked, usually beginning with, Why does that beer cost so much?

Time. Most ales only spend a few weeks at a brewery before departing. IPAs, they grow up so fast, don't they? Sour and wild beers are sort of like kids who take a little longer to realize their full potential, even if it means marinating on the couch for a couple of years, not paying rent, mooching from your bank account.

Lately, tart and tangy beers, in particular Germany's bracing Berliner weisse and salty and acidic gose, have become far more affordable. I'm talking around twelve dollars for canned six-packs of widely distributed beers such as Avery's margarita-like El Gose and Sierra Nevada's agave-and-lime gose, Otra Vez. The key to both the pucker and the lower price tag is a brewing process called kettle souring.

★ ★ ★

Advice: "When I first tasted a kettle sour my thought was 'pink champagne,' but after making my first one I realized the flavor mimicked sour candy. They are sour, bright, spritzy, and showcase fruit exceptionally well."

—Tonya Cornett, research and development brewmaster, 10 Barrel Brewing

★ ★ ★

WHY BREWERS PUT THEIR PEDAL TO THE KETTLE

How does kettle souring work? Well, brewers simmer grains in stainless steel mash tuns, or kettles, to create wort, the sugar-rich broth that becomes beer. Brewers sterilize the wort by briefly boiling it, then cool it down and add lactic acid bacteria, most commonly *Lactobacillus*. Over the next couple of days, the bacteria produce lactic acid that lowers the pH. When the beer reaches a brewery's preferred tartness, the liquid undergoes a second sterilization to kill the bacteria, and yeast is then pitched. *Voila!* That's sour beer on a super-fast timeline.

"The great thing about kettle sours is that they're relatively easy to make," says Firestone Walker's Richardson. "There's probably a little less risk." Souring bacteria and *Brettanomyces* have a nasty habit of hanging out where they're not wanted and causing havoc, like surly teens rampaging through a convenience store. "Not everybody has the luxury of a separate building where they can house barrels and lots of different microflora."

Time, convenience, and safety come at a cost. Beers patiently fermented with mixed cultures of yeast and bacteria are like a chorus, distinct voices singing in unison. By comparison, a kettle sour is a solo singer belting out a single unmistakable note: bright, lemony, and tart. "To me, they're very crisp, light, focused beers," Richardson says. "They live up to the name sours because it really is about the lactic acid."

While working as Bend Brewing's brewmaster, Tonya Cornett was one of the first brewers to experiment with kettle souring. She used the technique to create beers like the Berliner weisse–style Ching Ching, flavored with hibiscus and pomegranate. The method initially left her a little bashful. Wasn't this cheating? "During one Great American Beer Festival I had a conversation with Ron Jefferies of Jolly Pumpkin explaining the kettle sour I was pouring," says Cornett, now the research and development brewmaster at 10 Barrel Brewing. "I found myself apologizing for its lack of complexity. He asked why I was apologizing when this beer clearly hit the targets I had set out to achieve. From then on I started appreciating the simple beauty of these beers."

Kettle sours are rarely served unadulterated, no more complicated than lemon squeezed into seltzer. Breweries treat them as acidic blank slates, doctoring the beers with all manner of produce. For example, Cornett's Crush series of user-friendly kettle sours features everything from raspberries to kiwis and cucumbers, while many Florida breweries specialize in vibrantly hued "Florida weisse" sours. The Berliner weisse–inspired beers of J. Wakefield, Funky Buddha, 7venth Sun, and Coppertail contain the tropical likes of key limes, kumquats, and passion fruit.

"Kettle sours have an approachability factor that works well for the beginner sour drinker," Cornett says. "I believe that if you like sour candy, you are more likely to appreciate these beers. It is an easy flavor memory to tap into."

GOSE AND GUEUZE: YES, THERE IS A DIFFERENCE

★ ★ ★

Every day, perplexed beer drinkers everywhere wonder this: What's a gose, and why do some people spell it *gueuze*? Though the words seem *somewhat* similar, as if run through a malfunctioning translator, they are linguistically distinct. A gose ("goes-uh") is an ancient German beer that has undergone an American rebirth. Traditionally, the tart beer is seasoned with salt, an electrolyte-packed refresher that I'll glug over a sports drink anytime. By contrast, Belgium's dry, funky, and bubbly gueuze ("gooz") is a blend of one-, two-, and three-year-old lambic, a spontaneously fermented beer.

BREWED AWAKENING: "My major beer epiphany was tasting Bam Bière from Jolly Pumpkin. It was funky, tart, fruity, bitter, and had an indescribable rustic character. It played a major part in sending me down the rabbit hole of wild fermentation."

—Jeffrey Stuffings, founder and owner, Jester King Brewery

KISS FROM A ROSÉ: WHAT TO SERVE YOUR WINE-LOVING FRIENDS

Some nights, after I've spent a long day toiling in the verb-ridden mines of writing, my wife will come home from work and ask if there's anything to drink. I'll gesture to our hills of pilsners, IPAs, and stouts seasoned in bourbon-soaked oak. "Is there anything *I* can drink?" she'll ask again.

She sits pretty firmly on Team Wine, favoring dry whites in the crisp model of sauvignon blanc and Riesling. Some may see this as a nuclear bomb lobbed at our relationship's bedrock. I view it as a blessing (more beer for me!) and a free focus group to discover beers that wine lovers will love.

In particular, she gravitates toward gose. It's testament to the style's ability to reach across the beer aisle and shake hands with wine. "I have seen the reaction

Hibiscus flowers can lend beer a lovely pink tint and a touch of tartness.

of many people who have claimed 'I'm not a beer drinker' and 'I don't like beer,'" says Phil Markowski, the master brewer at Two Roads. "You get them to try it, and it's almost a universally pleasant response."

Inside former dairy tankers parked outside the Connecticut brewery, Markowski acidifies a wide range of goses, including one brewed with sauvignon blanc grapes. They deliver a lovely tropical nose, honeydew melon dancing with passion fruit and lime, and extend an invitation to wine drinkers: come on in, we're not so different.

Rosé-inspired beer is another lure to reel in wine drinkers. Fruity and floral rosé is firmly lodged in popular culture, a synonym for sun-soaked hedonism, and spawning memes like #yeswayrose. Breweries have taken note of the trend and released their own riffs on sparkling rosé, canned up for portable consumption anytime and everywhere. They appeal to beer lovers looking to sip something new, as well as wine fans wading into familiar waters.

★ ★ ★

Advice: Tired of murky, candy-sweet IPAs? Try their counterpoint, the dry and bubbly brut IPA, which takes its name from one of the driest categories of champagne. The key to the tinder-like profile is amylase, a brewing enzyme that converts starches into the simple sugar glucose that yeast readily devours, lessening residual sweetness.

★ ★ ★

★ ★ ★

Advice: "Beer-wine hybrids are literally the oldest known fermentable liquids. It's a captivating story, but it's also a great way to engage with wine lovers from the beer angle."

—Sam Calagione, founder and president, Dogfish Head Craft Brewed Ales

★ ★ ★

There are multiple paths to achieving that blushing tint. Sparkale from 21st Amendment is a "sparkling rosé ale" that stars peach, cherry, apple, and cranberry juices, while Firestone Walker's Rosalie is cofermented with chardonnay and other grape varietals and colored pink with hibiscus. Hoof Hearted's Rosé Gosé also contains hibiscus, plus pink Himalayan sea salt. "I know a lot of people into wine who dug it really hard," says Trevor Williams, a cofounder of the Columbus, Ohio, brewery. "We wanted to make a rosé-tasting beer that was much more crushable than rosé. You can definitely get in trouble drinking too much rosé too quickly."

Crooked Stave has found fierce demand for its canned Sour Rosé. The wild ale is fermented in big ol' oak foeders alongside raspberries and blueberries, equally fizzy, funky, and fruity. "It's our best-selling beer," says founder and brewmaster Chad Yakobson. That's right: six-packs of Sour Rosé are so popular that they even outsell Crooked Stave IPAs.

IT'S GREAT TO GO GRAPE

Five years ago, I believed that grape-infused beers would break big. The market was ripe with great hybrids like Cascade Brewing's tangy Vine, which is refermented with the juice of white wine grapes, or Captain Lawrence's richly vinous Rosso e Marrone, made with merlot and zinfandel grapes.

"When beer-wine hybrids were starting to get attention, it was mostly because they were so expensive to make because of the grape must," says Dogfish Head founder Sam Calagione, one of the earliest and biggest advocates of adding grapes to beer. "They were mostly sold in 750ml bottles because that drove home the connection to the wine world. That moment coincided

Amy Crook is the quality control manager for Firestone Walker.

Oregon's Alesong Brewing and Blending regularly incorporates local grapes into its beer.

with craft beer lovers leaning more into cans than big-bottle formats. That was just an unlucky packaging trend dovetailing with a really cool, great beer trend."

Now, beer-wine hybrids are poised to usher in new worlds of flavor, a familiar taste in a foreign setting. Dogfish Head's dryly fruity Viniferous IPA is fermented with Riesling and Viognier grape must, a beer fit for fans of white wine. Tired Hands' experimental Frequency Illusion series regularly features cofermentations with grapes, such as the Skin Contact variant made with merlot grapes grown in Pennsylvania. (It's reminiscent of Georgian orange wines.) Bruery Terreux, the Bruery's sour and wild offshoot, extensively explores the intersection of grapes and grain in beers such as Turo. It starts as a sour blonde that's aged on whole-cluster Grenache grapes, including stems, skins, and seeds, before the fruit is removed and pressed and the juice is added back to the beer to finish fermenting in oak. The garnet liquid was packaged still, a sour beer with the body and complexity of fine red wine. "The goal was to really take the wine and beer hybrid to an exceptional level," says Terreux production manager Jeremy Grinkey. "This is truly one of the most blurring-the-lines beer that has ever been made."

Matt Van Wyk, the brewmaster and a cofounder of Alesong Brewing and Blending, is bullish on the future of beer-wine hybrids. Alesong sits twenty miles southwest of Eugene, Oregon, right in the vine-covered heart of the Willamette Valley's wine country. "We're already using several kinds of Oregon fruit in our beers, so grapes seemed like another extension," Van Wyk says. Alesong's Terroir series of wine grape–matured farmhouse ales combined barrel aging, Willamette Valley fruit, and a host of microbes to create beers that deliver a distinct sense of place. (And medals. In 2018, two of Alesong's Terroir beers won Great American Beer Festival awards.)

"Wine has done a great job of telling the story of *terroir*—how the soil, sun, and everything that affects grapes' growth is reflected in wine," Van Wyk says. "With beer, people won't always believe you if you start to talk about *terroir*. When they see barley malted in Canada and hops coming from Washington and being shipped to New York, that's not a sense of place. When you're in wine country and you went down the road to your grape grower and picked those grapes, suddenly you have a sense of place. You've got an ingredient in beer that shows the *terroir*."

★ ★ ★

Fun Fact: Denver's Liberati Osteria and Oenobeers uses grapes and both winemaking equipment and methodologies to intertwine beer and wine in unexpected ways. It's time to drink tannic stouts made with 25 percent cabernet sauvignon grapes, or purposely oxidized beers that evoke aged port.

★ ★ ★

Van Wyk uses his tasting room to break people from belief systems. "When I have someone walk into my tasting room who would rather not drink beer and we hand them this purple-colored beer with aromas of grapes and tannins and wild yeast, suddenly they look at us with open eyes and say, 'That's not beer. It's delicious though.' To me, that's the mark of success when a customer just loves what you did. Then you say, 'Sit down, let me tell you the story of how we made that beer.'"

Beer and wine tend to sit in different mental silos, holding a different set of perceived values and worth. We don't have to tiptoe too far back in time to find

★ ★ ★

Fun Fact: I could never pronounce Willamette, the name of an Oregon region and hop variety, till I memorized this rhyming phrase: "It's Willamette, damn it."

★ ★ ★

Don't be surprised if these grapes are blended with beer.

Advice: "I believe brewers should make a wine-beer hybrid that tastes somewhat like wine but you know it's still a beer. You don't want so much grape flavor that it's like, 'This tastes like grape juice.'"

—Matt Van Wyk, brewmaster and cofounder, Alesong Brewing and Blending

a moment when wine was considered cheap plonk, brands like Thunderbird—a flavored fortified wine—immortalized in radio jingles.

"Wineries have done a remarkable job of marketing to their consumers why their wine costs what it does. In the beer world, we haven't done as great of a job. But when you meld the grapes in with the beer, you're suddenly doing things more like a winery and you can better tell a story," Van Wyk says. "When you explain it in terms of, 'It's just another alcoholic beverage,' then

Fun Fact: The word *wino* originated in the United States around 1915, the phrase derogatory slang for someone who drinks too much wine, particularly of the cheap sort.

it blurs the lines between wine and beer. Think of it as a beverage, not that this is beer and this is wine. It's a beverage that we're happy to make for you."

YEAST MODE: WHY NOVEL MICROBES ARE FERMENTING A FLAVORFUL REVOLUTION

It's easy to feel world-weary when walking down a beer aisle. Coffee porters, bourbon barrel–aged imperial stouts, double IPAs packed with trendy hops: bought this, drank that, no new ingredients under the sun. That's not quite the case. Some of the most novel ingredients are found under a microscope.

"In the best beers today, yeast is the star," says Chris White, the founder and president of White Labs.

Flavorings such as peppermint sticks and spruce tips are easy to comprehend. We can envision brewers lopping off a tree's branches and lobbing them into a simmering kettle. Beakers full of a single-celled organism offer less romance, like that year I gave my wife a plastic water bottle for her birthday. Though yeast is tiny, the strains contain multitudes of flavor, creating some of beer's most memorable profiles.

Yeast gives a traditional hefeweizen its famous aroma of cloves and bananas, no fruit required. Yeast gives a classic saison an earthy, spicy, and black-pepper complexity, no crack of the peppermill required. Historically, "there's nothing fruity in

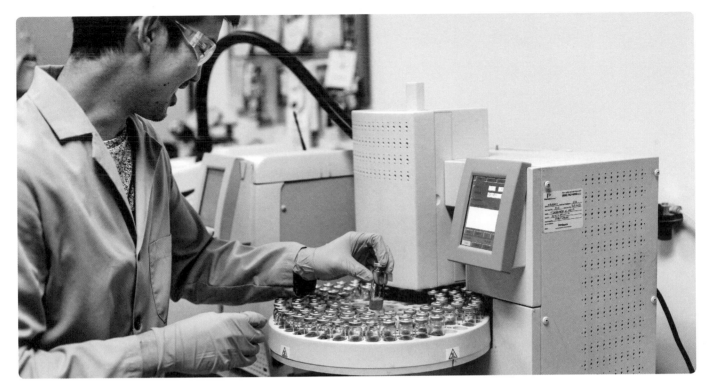

A technician at White Labs analyzes yeast samples.

hops or malt," White says. "Pretty much all of that comes from yeast."

White is one of America's preeminent fermentation specialists. He authored *Yeast: The Practical Guide to Beer Fermentation*, earned a PhD in biochemistry, and in 1995 founded White Labs, supplying yeast cultures for wineries, distilleries, and breweries. During modern brewing's foundational days in the 1980s and 1990s, distinct and dependable yeast strains were tough to find. Industrial-scale breweries handled yeast needs in house; fledgling breweries needed to look elsewhere for the yeast strains that would help them replicate the world's greatest styles.

"When the American craft brewers started, they were like, I want to make German beer, I want to make British beer, I want to make Belgian beer. This required strains that were native to those areas of the world," White says. "What was a small brewery supposed to do? There were going to be limited choices without new yeast labs to support them."

Yeast suppliers such as White Labs and Oregon's Wyeast Laboratories, which was founded in 1986, played critical, yet largely unheralded, roles in delivering breweries the living raw materials required to create memorable beer. We all sing the praises of hop farmers, bowing down at the agrarian altar

White Labs is one of the brewing industry's biggest suppliers of yeast.

of Citra and Mosaic. But scientists and researchers also deserve rounds of clapping, for they're helping steer beer in delicious new directions. "There are around 1,500 known species of yeast, but that's not very many," White says. "There are still a lot more out there in the wild."

On the Hunt

Hunting for yeast is kind of a crapshoot. Simply capturing a strain is no guarantee that it's going to be any good at fermenting beer. Several years ago, a few brewing friends brought some wort to a bygone Brooklyn brewery, where the 1850s lagering caves sit thirty feet beneath the city streets. Today, Crown Finish Caves uses the underground tunnels to age cheese, microflora permeating most every brick. It seemed like a solid bet that the tunnels would yield glorious yeast, but the results were blah—a starry-eyed vision crashing into cold-hearted reality.

"Every week we're trialing new yeast strains," says White, whose company regularly canvasses different geographical regions to gather yeast. "[In 2018], we did a lot of collections around North and South Carolina. We're looking for some jewel in there. There are so many great yeasts out there, but many of them don't have the brewing properties. You try to find strains in the wild that might be close."

You never know when, or where, you'll discover a rule-breaking strain. Dr. Matt Bochman, a founder of Indiana's Wild Pitch Yeast, collected a sample from the bark of an ash tree in his dad's backyard. To his surprise, the yeast created lactic acid without the aid of souring bacteria. "That's not a characteristic that regular *Saccharomyces* or *Brettanomyces* or any other brewing yeast creates," says Eric Anderson, the brewmaster at Cleveland, Ohio's Saucy Brew Works. It was the first brewery to experiment with what Wild Pitch called YH72, creating a blonde ale.

"You'll notice it's a sour beer for sure, but it's much more rounded and mellower," Anderson says. "It's not sharp." Sour Blonde is part of Saucy's Drifter Series dedicated to beers that don't fit into neat little categories. "Technically, it's a new style of beer that we're calling a yeast-only sour."

★ ★ ★

Fun Fact: Here's your golden opportunity to drink beer in underground lagering tunnels. Brooklyn's Crown Finish Caves runs the bimonthly Cave Music series, partnering musicians with cheese and locally brewed beer (crownfinishcaves.com).

★ ★ ★

THE KVEIK AND THE DELICIOUS

Personally, I'm stoked about the category-exploding potential of Norway's quirky kveik, a yeast primed for our IPA-addled times. (Say "kwike," which translates to "yeast" in a specific Norwegian dialect.)

Traditionally, kveik was a family heirloom passed down from generation to generation, customarily stored on woven straw rings, linen, or pieces of wood with drilled holes. The Norwegian farmhouse yeast refuses to follow a rulebook. Most yeast strains favor fairly rigid temperature ranges, some cooler, some warmer. Roam too far from their happy place, and yeast will get more stressed than me trying to write another book. The beleaguered fungi will start producing off flavors like bandages and rotting garbage.

Pittsburgh's Cinderlands Beer uses the Norwegian yeast kveik in numerous beers.

THE COOL WAY TO STAND APART

In a world where nearly every brewery has access to the same hops, grains, and store-bought yeast strains, spontaneous fermentations let brewers stand apart in an ever-crowded field. This might be beer's last wide-open frontier. "There's still a lot of fresh ground to cover," says James Watt, a cofounder of BrewDog. The brewery's offshoot OverWorks facility in Scotland, contains a copper coolship—imagine a massive rectangular baking pan—that brewers fill with steamy wort, then open the windows and let local microbes flutter in and settle in for a feast. The hope is that the native microorganisms will create beers with a distinct taste. In the beer of Black Project Spontaneous and Wild Ales, "we have a certain candied-peach characteristic that comes through at one time or another," cofounder James Howat says. "It's subtle. It's not like a peach beer. It's not something that you can reproduce in a lab." These five great coolship-equipped breweries charmingly embrace spontaneity.

⋆ ⋆ ⋆

Beachwood Blendery (Long Beach, California): Since 2015, the SoCal brewery's focused mission has been to reproduce true-to-tradition facsimiles of lambics and gueuzes, right down to mimicking the temperature and humidity of barrel rooms in Belgium.

De Garde Brewing (Tillamook, Oregon): Founders Trevor and Lindsay Rogers specifically selected this coastal Oregon town for its indigenous yeast and microflora. Pacific Ocean breezes bring in the bugs that inoculate every beer, including its "The" series of lambic-inspired beers that champion regional grains, hops, and fruit.

Funk Factory Geuzeria (Madison, Wisconsin): Instead of brewing, Levi Funk totes a coolship to different midwestern breweries to source wort.

The spontaneously fermented liquid becomes beers like the lemony Meerts, lambic's younger, low-alcohol sibling.

OEC Brewing (Oxford, Connecticut): Be it aging barrels underground or in unheated barns, importer B. United's standalone brewery investigates the eccentric fringes of brewing. OEC makes extensive usage of its coolship in its rustic gose, Salsus, and Berliner weisse–style Exilis.

Oxbow Brewing Company (Newcastle, Maine): When the weather cools at the rural farmhouse brewery, Oxbow brews batches of beer with native grains and well water to fill the outdoor coolship and create Native/Wild, an undiluted taste of Maine.

The outdoor coolship at Maine's Oxbow Brewing.

Kveik has a hardier constitution. The farmhouse yeast will gladly function whether the thermometer reads seventy or nearly one hundred degrees Fahrenheit. "Our first thought was, 'They're either making god-awful beer in Norway, or these are special strains,'" says Lance Shaner, a cofounder of Chicago's Omega Yeast. "If you were to take an English ale strain and ferment it at such high temperatures, it would taste like jet fuel."

Norway's Lars Marius Garshol, an expert in farmhouse beer, sent Omega a sample for testing. The yeast proved to be a magical wunderkind: it worked well at elevated temperatures, creating intense aromas of tropical fruit—the perfect stage for modern IPAs.

"If we use the kveik yeast and combine them with hops, it gives us a whole new world and platform to build fruit flavors," says Paul Schneider, the head brewer at Pittsburgh's Cinderlands Beer. "Kveik lends a little bit of residual sweetness to support the fruit flavors that come out of the fermentation and hops. A little bit of sweetness really makes our beer taste super-fat and sticky and juicy and ripe."

Schneider is so hooked on kveik that he exclusively ferments all of his hazy IPAs with the Norwegian yeast.

★ ★ ★

Fun Fact: Amateur and commercial brewers can buy different strains of kveik from suppliers including the Yeast Bay and Omega Yeast, including the latter's HotHead Ale. It creates an aroma reminiscent of ripe mangos and honey.

★ ★ ★

"It takes things into a new territory and it's super-exciting for me. I can't wait to see what other brewers do with this," he says. "These kveik yeasts can definitely be the stars of the show."

★ ★ ★

Fun Fact: Norwegian farmhouse ales take top billing at fall's Norsk Kornolfestival, a festival in western Norway that features scores of beer fermented with kveik and infused with traditional ingredients including juniper berries and branches (norskkornolfestival.no).

★ ★ ★

BREWED AWAKENING: "I didn't enjoy beer for a good portion of my life. The bland mass-produced brands offered nothing more than grainy bitterness that I did not find enjoyable, so I mostly stuck with cider and cocktails. But in 1999, I landed in Germany for a DJ gig and a friend greeted me with a Berliner weisse. The acidity sang to me and opened my eyes to what beer is, and can be. From there I went on a search to explore the world of funky beer like Belgian lambics and farmhouse ales that eventually led me to produce my own hybridized styles based on these obscure offerings' foundations, but designed for my personal tastes."

—Brian Strumke, founder, Stillwater Artisanal Ales

SEEING THE LIGHT (BEER)

You might assume that IPAs have conquered every crook and bend of the beer landscape, but America's top-selling beers remain light lagers: Bud Light followed by Coors Light, with Budweiser and Miller Lite neck and neck in third place. "We're all trying to sell craft to craft, and we're all fighting for the same space," says Founders Brewing CEO Mike Stevens. "It's getting more competitive." To reach the masses craving low-alcohol beers that refresh without wrecking taste buds or budgets, Founders and other brewers now offer light-drinking lagers. "Most consumers out there are not drinking craft," Stevens says. "Why can't we sell beer to that demographic?" Here are four tastier takes on the crowd-pleasing, cooler-filling lager.

✦ ✦ ✦

Alvarado Street Brewery: Buzz Light Beer (4.5 percent ABV)
Brewed with the yeast used to make Germany's Augustiner lager, the helles-style Buzz pairs bubbles aplenty with a bready character.

Firestone Walker Brewing: Firestone Lager (4.5 percent ABV)
The light-bodied lager was first brewed in 2000, a classic case of being ahead of the curve. Firestone revived the brand in 2018, using German hops for a floral, herbal hit.

Founders Brewing: Solid Gold (4.4 percent ABV)
Lemondrop hops give the corn-packed crusher a subtle hint of citrus that helps it stand out from the pack, as does its price: around fifteen dollars for a fifteen-pack of 12-ounce cans.

Night Shift Brewing: Nite Lite (4.3 percent ABV)
The unfiltered Lite tastes like a tailgate session, but better. I like buying it by the 16-ounce tallboy.

Easygoing lagers like Solid Gold, from Founders, are making a play for mainstream drinkers.

THE GREAT AMERICAN ZERO

I never really saw a reason to drink a nonalcoholic beer. Most tasted pretty meh, missing not just booze but flavor as well. Just pass me the seltzer, please. But now there's competition for cans of LaCroix. Breweries are fashioning nonalcoholic (NA) IPAs, stouts, and wheat beers, finding a thirsty market of athletes, baby boomers, and others eager to explore a universe of flavor, no hangover included. "If you drink alcohol, your choices are unlimited," says Jeff Stevens. "If you don't, they aren't."

Stevens quit drinking when he was twenty-four, somewhat ironically spending several decades in beer-industry marketing. "I understood this market in the sense that there are not a lot of good NA beers," he says. To fix that, Stevens launched the Saint Louis–based, NA-focused WellBeing Brewing in 2018. He hired O'Fallon Brewery to contract-brew a dark amber ale and a Blue Moon–inspired wheat beer, the alcohol removed via vacuum distillation. WellBeing beers retain aroma and flavor, offering folks a taste of what they never knew they were missing. "I had no idea what a hop-forward anything was," Stevens says. "It's so much fun to try these styles."

WellBeing received an unexpected boost during the 2018 winter Olympics when news broke that German Olympians drink NA beer during training, using it as a nutrient-rich sports drink. "What I loved about the Olympics story is that it wasn't just the polyphenols that were good for you, it was the sociability of beer," Stevens says. "That's something you're never going to get in a sports drink."

WellBeing Brewing specializes in nonalcoholic beer.

Philip Brandes still drinks alcohol, but after a buddy went sober, the software developer challenged himself to brew a great alcohol-free IPA. "I'm really good at seeing a problem and working on it," he says. Brandes, who lives in Southern California, bought equipment and became obsessed. "My wife was like, 'Yeah, you're going to need to write this stuff off and start a brewery,'" he says, laughing.

He founded Bravus Brewing in June 2016, his oatmeal stout, amber ale, and Pliny the Elder—inspired IPA created via a proprietary process featuring specialized yeast and an app-controlled brewing system. He thought folks like his freshly sober friend would be the prime takers, but he soon tapped a fresh consumer artery. "The majority of our demographic are boomers or seniors. They want a healthier lifestyle or want to get into craft beer," he says.

His accounts buck the mold. One Saint Patrick's Day, Brandes delivered two kegs of green-dyed IPA to a senior community called Leisure World. Moreover, Brandes can distribute his booze-free beer to places that lack liquor licenses, be it food trucks, delis, or individual consumers in all fifty states. "I can sell in a lot of places that standard beer can't," he says. Bravus fast outgrew its first space, then a second, and now it rents space from larger breweries. "I can't make the stuff fast enough," he says, adding that people preorder beer several months in advance. "It's almost like a can-release line for NA beer."

Craft brewers are starting to pay attention. Mikkeller makes an alcohol-free beer spiced with orange peel and coriander, while Brooklyn Brewery has the Special Effects hoppy lager. Sweden's Omnipollo is famed for high-test imperial stouts and IPAs, but it's boomeranging back to the opposite end of the spectrum. "This is just as radical, if not even more," cofounder and brewer Henok Fentie says of exploring alcohol-free beer.

The dad of three sees the role that NA beer can play in his life. "When it's zero, it might be because

I'm driving or I'm not keen going down that route that evening," he says. "Zero fits into consumer behavior because it has a purpose."

⭐ ⭐ ⭐

Fun Fact: Two words: hard seltzer (see page 104). Look for breweries to increasingly frolic in this spritzy arena, creating Zima—a clearly sparkling 1990s novelty—for a new generation.

⭐ ⭐ ⭐

BREWED AWAKENING: "I thought it was really cool when I was in university and I drank Bass Ale. It was like I was drinking history. I was taking in that whole British vibe of ale culture. That really filled the void. I grew up on Schmidt's, Grain Belt, and Pabst. I thought it was pretty snarky for me to jump over and get into Bass Ale. Then Anchor Steam hit me upside the head and I was introduced to Augsburger, a fairly hopped lager made by this little brewery in Monroe, Wisconsin. Those two experiences led me to homebrewing. I was so full of myself I thought, 'Why don't I just make barley wines and imperial pilsners at home?'"

—Mark Stutrud, founder and president, Summit Brewing

TIME TO GET ATHLETIC

★ ★ ★

In my office, you'll find a miniature fridge filled with more beer than any one human should responsibly drink. My canned and bottled coworkers offer endless temptations. They whisper, *Wouldn't a little mood adjustment help you finish that article?* Reader, it may amaze you that I'm not drunk from daylight to dusk. But I do like a good beer. And for that I turn to Athletic Brewing. The Connecticut brewery makes some of my favorite nonalcoholic beers, including the light and floral Upside Dawn golden ale and the tropically leaning Run Wild IPA. "For decades, nonalcoholic beer was an afterthought of marketing departments and innovation teams," says founder Bill Shufelt. "Athletic has a team of highly awarded brewers crafting a wide range of styles in a dedicated brewery." Maybe you'll never make it to their tasting room, but that's no big deal. The best thing about nonalcoholic beer is that there's no FOMO: you can buy it online (athleticbrewing.com/shop).

Go on, drink a six-pack and skate around the rink. Athletic's beers are booze-free.

For Fentie, flavor is the ultimate arbiter: "I won't drink 10 zero-percent beers just because it has less alcohol." The beer must be as delicious as, say, Omnipollo's porter that's reminiscent of rocky road ice cream. The brewery spent a year developing Konx, a nonalcoholic "mini pale" that can stand its ground with standard-strength pale ales in the taste department.

"Nonalcoholic beer must be a viable alternative in terms of flavor," he says. "Otherwise you can drink something else that's really tasty, like ginseng tea."

DRINKING DESTINATION

London: Where Beer's Past Is Served Up alongside Its Future

Will Hawkes, veteran British beer journalist

★ ★ ★

Author Will Hawkes.

When Derek Prentice began his brewing career at Truman's in 1968, London was a city of large Victorian breweries and street-corner pubs. Now railway-arch breweries and trading-estate taprooms define its beer scene, though some things haven't changed. London is still a drinker's city, and no one knows that better than Prentice. "I think I'm not bad at drinking," he said to loud laughter at the recent celebrations for his half century in brewing. "I can hold my own."

London has one foot in the past and one in the future. No other city in the world has such a rich blend, although Londoners tend to be fairly conservative when it comes to what they choose to drink. Having written about London's beer scene for more than ten years, for publications ranging from the *Washington Post* to the *Guardian*, I've seen the emergence of a diverse and often experimental beer scene, but it's still honest-to-goodness session beer that puts bread on brewers' tables here.

I recently spoke to the owner of a chain of craft-beer pubs who told me that 70 percent of their sales were Camden Hells, a 4.6 percent ABV pale lager brewed in the Bavarian tradition. (It's very good.) Brewers like the Kernel, meanwhile, sell far more of their hoppy pale ales than anything else. (They're very good, too.)

And if you walk into the Harp, perhaps central London's best spot for beer, on a Friday evening, you'll get an unforgettable taste of cask-ale culture, with customers three-deep at the bar and staff assiduously pulling perfectly kept beers. (Cask ale, the ultimate session beer, can be a lottery elsewhere in London; best to try before you buy.)

(continued on next page)

London pub culture remains an integral part of the country's drinking culture.

This adherence to beer-swilling tradition can be frustrating for London's 120-odd breweries (only one of which, Fuller's, existed twenty-five years ago). Restaurants in London have been slow to catch on to beer's potential, probably because it does not offer the same margin as wine, although that's changing. Craft-beer bars, too, are thinner on the ground than you'd expect, almost certainly because Londoners prefer to drink in pubs; an exception is the excellent Mother Kelly's, in Bethnal Green and Vauxhall, where a well-chosen variety of modern beers from Britain and beyond draws a young crowd.

By contrast, there are many great pubs. Two favorites are the Pembury Tavern, the recently renovated brewery tap for Five Points in East London, where a pint of Railway Porter goes perfectly with a game of bar billiards, and the Royal Oak, one of two pubs owned by Sussex brewery Harvey's in London. Here you'll find the best of the past: cask-conditioned mild, a jar of pickled eggs on the bar, and an atmosphere of unhurried contentment.

In upper-crust West London, meanwhile, the many Fuller's pubs are your best bet: follow former head brewer John Keeling's advice and don't judge London Pride until the third pint.

A recent growth industry has been taprooms, particularly in Tottenham and Bermondsey. The latter has become the de facto capital of modern London beer: on Saturday mornings, with nearly all of its breweries open to the public, it is the city's most popular pub crawl. Don't miss Fourpure, whose beer is consistently excellent, or Brew by Numbers, where innovation and drinkability go hand in hand.

For a brewery that straddles the gap between old and new London, though, it's hard to look beyond Derek Prentice's current employer, Wimbledon. On a cold October afternoon, to celebrate his fiftieth year in beer, he tapped a cask of XXXX, a barley wine that weighs in at more than 10 percent ABV. It's not a session beer by any stretch of the imagination, but it was so smooth and rich that you could forgive many of the attendees for forgetting that.

Mother Kelly's is one of London's best modern beer bars.

HIGH HOPES: THE FUTURE OF MARIJUANA AND BEER

America has always had a knotty relationship with drugs and alcohol. Intoxicants have been demonized and celebrated depending on the decade and the direction of the political winds. Let's stroll down a deeply intoxicated memory lane.

Druggists in the nineteenth century sold Mrs. Winslow's Soothing Syrup, a morphine-laced pain reliever ("the mother's friend for children teething," read one advertisement), while in 1890 Allen's Cocaine Tablets purportedly cured "nervousness, headache, and sleeplessness." (I'll let that one sink in for a second.) In 1896 customers could even order vials of cocaine and powdered opium from the Sears, Roebuck catalog—the proto-Amazon of its era—while in 1901 Bayer marketed heroin as the "cheapest specific for the relief of coughs."

Our good-times friend alcohol also endured a thirteen-year stretch of illicitness, a little period called Prohibition. Remember it? Probably not! (For all my octogenarian and nonagenarian readers, welcome.) Our lives are governed by laws and molded by experience. I've existed in a reality in which alcohol and homebrewing are legal, while marijuana is illegal. Right and wrong, light and dark.

Now, those distinctions are fast going up in smoke. State by state, America is marching toward a reality where marijuana and beer legally coexist, Bud served with a side of bud. This has left the brewing industry in a slight tizzy. "I think the big question mark for me

SweetWater Brewing's 420 Strain G13 IPA is inspired by marijuana.

is, How many disposable dollars will people have to spend on all of these different products that are used to accomplish a similar goal: being inebriated or not being entirely sober?" says Chris Furnari, the editor of *Brewbound*.

Where There Isn't Smoke, There's Beer

Breweries aren't twiddling their thumbs at the end of the bench while people speed-walk to their local dispensary for some joints and gummies. Looming legalization presents a fortunes-altering opportunity for brewers and beverage makers to write a new future for cannabis and beer, a link that's not such an odd couple: Marijuana and hops are members of the *Cannabaceae* family of flowering plants, and they offer similar olfactory experiences. In other words, there's a reason that some IPAs smell as dank as strains of high-grade marijuana.

At Ceria Brewing, Blue Moon Belgian White creator Keith Villa creates THC-infused non-alcoholic beer.

"We're at a time where it's very similar to when alcohol prohibition was repealed," says Keith Villa, the former head brewmaster at MillerCoors. "It's kind of the birth and the start of this new era. It's a situation that comes around once in a lifetime."

Or twice, for some people. In the mid-1990s, Villa created Blue Moon Belgian White. The cloudy and citrusy wheat beer, often served with an orange slice, became a blockbuster that helped introduce flavorful beer to a broader marketplace. Disrupting the beverage industry and building a strong brand are two strengths that will suit him well at Ceria Brewing.

His new company makes THC-infused non-alcoholic beer, including Grainwave Belgian-Style White Ale, which contains 5mg of THC per 10-ounce serving. (The federal government legally forbids companies from mixing alcohol and THC.) The beverage shares a similar onset time to alcohol, meaning you'll feel effects in as few as eight or nine minutes. "In the early days of craft beer, there were a lot of people that jumped in and thought they could make a quick buck," Villa says. "We're going to be as careful as possible." Ceria's cannabis extracts are tasteless (in a good way!), centering the focus on beer flavor and THC's mood adjustment. "One thing that we learned quickly is that the smell and taste of cannabis is really polarizing," Villa says. "People either love it or they hate it. It's really dividing."

Mixing marijuana and beer does not require a kumbaya moment in which we sit by a campfire and

Nowadays, 5 p.m. means it's time to crack a . . . non-alcoholic, THC-infused beer from Two Roots Brewing.

all agree to never disagree. You can think this is a terrible, terrible thing, church and state served up by the 16-ounce can. That's understandable. What gets me is the creativity that I see. Browse a California dispensary and you might find Lagunitas Brewing's Hi-Fi Hops, a hoppy sparkling water that's topped off with THC, or Two Roots Brewing's range of alcohol-free, THC-dosed beers, including a stout, blonde ale, and IPA. Bars far and wide serve New Belgium's Hemperor HPA, made with hemp hearts, and SweetWater Brewing's 420 Strain G13 IPA. The sticky and resinous ale replicates the aromatics of G13, a notorious marijuana strain, but minus the THC. "It definitely has that high-grade cannabis flavor," says SweetWater cofounder Freddy Bensch.

Along with hops, the key ingredients are terpenes, a word you'll probably see bandied about a bunch in the coming days and years. Terpenes are the organic compounds that give everything from pine trees to lemons, hops, cannabis, and your backyard grass their signature scents. "This is next-generation stuff, right? This is a new world," Bensch says. "To bring those two occasions together in one product is phenomenal. We're embracing it."

For producers, there's no handy map to navigating these murky waters where a pot of gold may loom somewhere in the distance. Massive beverage companies including Molson Coors Canada and Constellation Brands, the Corona importer and Ballast Point owner, have committed resources to exploring the buzzy category. (Heineken, too, as the company owns Lagunitas.) Thirty years ago, nobody could've conceived a future where folks freely line up at nine o'clock in the morning for triple IPAs socked with pineapples or strawberries. Who knows, maybe one day we'll all spend our Sundays watching football games, toasting touchdowns with another round of nonalcoholic, THC-infused beers. Tomorrows are uncertain until we take a whack at new things today.

"We don't where it's going, but there's no harm in trying this stuff," says Gerry Khermouch, the editor of *Beverage Business Insights*. "Minds are open."

⬢

CBD IN BEER

★ ★ ★

Of late, the cannabis by-product cannabidiol, better known as CBD, has been touted as a cure-all for a wide range of maladies, the latest wellness-industry wonder ingredient. The medical jury may still be out on the compound's efficacy, but a number of breweries, including Portland's Coalition Brewing and Vermont's Long Trail, have explored blending CBD with beer. Will this be the future? Maybe. It sort of depends on how you want to take your medicine. "To me, CBD is a functional ingredient, and there is a large and growing user base of people that are using that product for sleep apnea and aches and joint pains," says Chris Furnari, the editor of *Brewbound*. "It's very functional. I just don't know where alcohol fits into that."

DR. J. NIKOL JACKSON-BECKHAM

Diversity ambassador, Brewers Association

★ ★ ★

In the '80s and '90s, America's maverick brewers broke the color barrier by brewing anything but foamy yellow lager. Amber ales, onyx stouts, and tawny IPAs were colorful and flavorful salvos against the prevailing state of fermented affairs. Today, a Pantone color guide could double as a beer list, a rainbow of tones and tastes available on tap. Historically, however, the brewers and drinkers themselves have been pretty monochromatic, the color of a quart of milk—this writer included.

Beards, flannels, basements, white dudes: the big-bellied stereotypes of beer are finally fraying. Beer is entering a more diverse and accepting era, one in which all kinds of skin colors and sexual orientations are finding entry points to enjoying IPAs and barrel-aged

Dr. J. Nikol Jackson-Beckham is the diversity ambassador for the Brewers Association industry trade group.

stouts, as well as brewing them. One of the leading voices of this multipronged, multicultural awakening is Dr. J. Nikol Jackson-Beckham, the diversity ambassador for the Brewers Association industry trade group.

"Anecdotally, I absolutely believe that there's a correlation between diversity of available styles and diversity of people who come to drink them," says Dr. Jackson-Beckham, who is also an assistant professor of communication studies at Randolph College, in Lynchburg, Virginia. In her role, she crisscrosses America to meet with state brewing guilds, attend beer conferences, deliver keynote addresses, and create dialogue about thoughtfully cultivating more diverse workplaces and clientele.

"I know a lot of times people are like, 'Ugh, god, one more thing. Let's not have one more high-pitched, high-stakes conversation,'" she says. "'Can't we just leave beer alone?' I understand that, but my answer is no. I'm just like, 'No, no you can't.'"

Dr. Jackson-Beckham's academic background helps her bring valuable and overlooked historical perspectives to conversations. "Americans are a vastly ahistorical people," she says. "When I talk about diversity and inclusion, I can say, 'Let's stop talking about whose fault anything is. This is a really stupid way to think about this.'"

Nothing occurs in a vacuum. There are causes, connections, and antecedents, the past delivering clues about the present day. "When people are like, 'Why is craft beer so white right now?' I'm like, 'Do you really want to talk about Jim Crow?' We've got to go far back to talk about why the industry is structured the way it's structured now," she says. "You be an African-American

in 1960 and try to get a bank loan for a business that has no precedent for operation. That's why it's never happened."

Dr. Jackson-Beckham has been deep in beer for more than two decades, starting with working at a sports bar in the late '90s while attending Virginia Tech, a drinking education one shift after another. Her interest steadily grew after graduation: a membership to a beer-of-the-month club, visits to bars and brewpubs, and a 2003 move to brewery-rich San Diego. There she fed her hobby with homebrewing, festivals, tours, beer dinners, a pastime blossoming into an obsession. By the time she returned to the East Coast in 2007, to attend the University of North Carolina at Chapel Hill, beer was big on her brain.

She worked at a gardening- and homebrew-supply shop, teaching classes (she favors maibocks, porters, and malt-forward reddish ales) and getting a nuts-and-bolts look at the brewing industry. "That big-picture view caught my attention as an academic," she says. "This is a big, big industrial formation that has these really involved cultural formations laid over it." She resolved to write her dissertation about the culture of beer, a move that looked like steering her career into a ditch. "My doctoral advisor made me promise that I wouldn't be mad at him if I never got a job," she says, laughing. "It took a lot of convincing. Why in the world would somebody getting a doctorate in communications studies write something about beer? It seemed insane, but it's less insane now."

(continued on next page)

In her role, Dr. Jackson-Beckham serves as a sounding board and orator of sound advice. Encouraging diversity doesn't mean creating on-the-nose events under the banner of inclusivity. (LGBTQ beer night! Multicultural happy hour!) "One of the big things I say is, 'Stop thinking that you have to be an organizer.' The questions are always, 'What should we do? What events should we have?' You should get out of the way," Dr. Jackson-Beckham says. "Humans are social creatures. We already get together. The question is, 'Are you savvy enough or open enough to make relationships or build partnerships with people that are already being collective?'"

The old ways of selling a single beer style to the masses are over. Today's brewers are trying anything and everything, creating pathways of flavor that entice consumers to wander down a new road. "The industry will have enough robustness and breadth to accommodate whomever," Dr. Jackson-Beckham says.

Niches, though, are inevitable. Craft beer was once a collection of offbeat islands in a sea of conformity, weird havens that felt like home. Now, double IPAs are sold at gas stations, grocery stores, and baseball stadiums, and identifying as a beer enthusiast has lost its anti-mainstream edge. Drinking tasty beer is just what people do every day, nothing special about it. So beer fans are bifurcating. Beer festivals now cater to devotees of heavy metal and hip-hop, or maybe they focus on female brewers. Find your tribe, and you'll find likeminded folks to share beer and conversation. Beer, though, should not be another wedge to drive people apart.

"When I lived in San Diego, there was a bar where I used to hang out. They had a couple different social beer groups who happened to meet at the same time on Sunday evening. There were a group of knitters, a group of board game people, and a tasting group. The cool part was that there were niches, but we could all see each other," Dr. Jackson-Beckham says. "I love the niches, but I want to make sure that the wall between my niche and your niche is maybe a foot high and we can talk about how fun it is to look across it."

★ ★ ★

EPILOGUE

could really go for a beer right now, and I don't have to go far. The refrigerator near my desk contains scores of cans and bottles, a dedicated beer depot to keep my IPAs from mingling with my family's condiments and milk. It's a very niche first-world problem, as is this one: deciding on my near-nightly beer.

Ten years ago, I was passionate to the point of obsession in my pursuit of the latest and highest-rated liquids. I stalked saisons, IPAs, and bourbon-barreled stouts as obsessively as a die-hard deer hunter, hoping to bag beer's biggest, most elusive bucks. Consuming Russian River's Pliny the Elder double IPA or the Bruery's Black Tuesday imperial stout felt momentous, a validation of my standing as a True Beer Connoisseur™.

I ventured to the far reaches of flavor country to drink up whatever brewers dreamed up. Sour, bitter, salty, sweet, chocolaty, fruity—I tried it all, thumbing my nose at mainstream lagers. Drinking Coors was uncouth, I believed, as déclassé as double-fisting cold, limp fries and guzzling flat Mountain Dew. *The horror. The horror!*

Fresh converts are always the most fanatical, aren't they?

Few fixations can go ninety miles per hour forever. My beer-questing mania has decelerated into a deep interest that's governed by a firm understanding of my palate's pleasure points. Those years of trying so many beers were, in hindsight, almost like a giant fishing expedition. Instead of hard-to-get trophy fish, I was really casting about for flavors, styles, and approaches that resonated with my mind, mouth, and lifestyle.

Today, my beer fridge's permanent residents stay steady: pilsners, moderate-strength IPAs, and an assortment of lagers, from toasty Vienna lagers to glass longnecks of Miller High Life consumed absent a side of irony. I'll still gladly try that yuzu-infused malted-milkshake IPA because, hey, you only live once. But the curiosities and proof-of-concept beers rarely stay in steady rotation.

Ten years ago, I probably would've bashfully admitted to liking High Life. It didn't fit the profile of the True Beer Connoisseur™. The line splitting craft and corporate brewers was clearly defined. Did I want fermented anarchy or status quo suds? Choosing sides was simple. Now it's hard. The dividing line isn't merely blurry; it's been run through a paper shredder and reassembled by a drunken cartographer. Anheuser-Busch InBev now owns Goose Island, Elysian, and Wicked Weed, among other breweries once clearly considered craft. Investments from venture-capital firms are commonplace. *Craft* has lost its linguistic cachet and is now a nothing burger on par with *artisanal*.

Increasingly, beer is no longer bought on flavor and taste alone. They're just two of the sundry decisions that consumers may take into consideration: independent versus corporate, local versus outsider, rarity versus ubiquity, cost versus cost. Does a brewery traffic in sexist or insensitive labels? Can a brewery's employees earn a living wage? What about a brewery's commitment to a community?

The calculus is complex because beer becomes entwined with us, both physically and emotionally. You're buying more than a fermented beverage. You're purchasing a brewery's worldview, a series of deliberate decisions made by people no different from you and me. Or your fellow beer fans. There's no reason to be elitist about imbibing. We all exist at different stages on our beer-drinking journey. You may have rounded Pastry Stout Mountain and the Valley of Mixed Fermentation, finding a nice plot of land on the Pilsner Plains. Other people might be exploring Blue Moon or be happily lost in the dry-hopped fog of Haze Town. That's OK. Travel long enough and you'll find agreeable roosts to call home, sometimes for a night, sometimes for the rest of your life.

Now I'm ready for that beer, and it's no fun to drink alone. What are you having? This refrigerator isn't going to empty itself.

ACKNOWLEDGMENTS

Books don't appear fully formed on bookshelves like some literary immaculate conception. Shepherding words and images to their final form takes a dedicated team of people who, most likely, have never shared beers on a Friday night, much less met in person. Modern life is a weird bird stuffed with emails.

Endless thanks go to the Sterling Publishing team for putting up with so many of mine. To start, Alexandra Brodsky gets huge high-fives for helping source the book's excellent images. (As I've always said, few people glance at a book and compliment your word choices.) Next, Gavin Motnyk did a bang-up job on the book design, the pages flowing together smoother than a stream of molten chocolate. On the editing tip, James Jayo handled the project in its embryonic stages, and then John Meils took the book kicking and screaming into the world. (Also: no kicking and screaming occurred.)

When writing in my home office got too lonely, my only friend the hissing radiator, coffee shop and beer hall Berg'n proved the perfect writing perch.

Thanks for letting me nurse a single cortado for hours, furiously clacking my keyboard like a deranged pianist. Equal cheers go to my neighborhood bottle shop and bar Covenhoven, where I spent endless afternoons sitting by the front window and sipping a pilsner, staring into the middle distance and conjuring up similes, metaphors, and dad-worthy puns, cackling quietly to myself.

To the brewers, bar owners, sensory specialists, professors, chefs, and other brainy beer experts, massive kudos for taking time to talk and never once telling me I say the word *um* too many times during interviews. Extra-special thanks to Allagash for arranging for me to spend a day meandering through the brewery, putting up with me as I (incorrectly) kept insisting that batches of White didn't taste right.

And to steer this gratitude bus into the garage, hugs and kisses go to my wife, Jenene, and daughter, Violet, for the support on the home front. When a five-year-old uses the right tone of voice, "poop dad" can sound just like a term of endearment.

GLOSSARY

Adjunct Fermentable substances that are substituted for the cereal grains (chiefly barley) that comprise beer. Adjuncts, such as rice and corn, can lighten a beer's body. That said, *adjunct* may seem like an evil word, but deployed judiciously, adjuncts can create killer beer.

Alcohol This mood-brightening by-product of fermentation occurs when yeasts devour sugars in the wort. Alcohol is measured in two categories: alcohol by volume (ABV) and alcohol by weight (ABW). In craft brewing, ABV is the standard measurement, but here's a quick tip on how to convert ABW to ABV: multiply by 1.25. Alcohol is about 80 percent the weight of water, making a 6 percent ABV beer about 4.8 percent ABW.

Ale One of two big families of beer, the other being lager. Ale yeasts favor warmer temperatures, hanging out at the top of a fermentation tank. An ale's flavors and aromas are typically a touch estery—that is, fruity—and can be sweeter and fuller-bodied than lagers. Ales encompass an enormous grab bag of styles, from imperial stouts to Belgian tripels and, yes, India pale ales.

Alpha acids Found in the hop cone, alpha acids contribute bitterness to beer. They are water-insoluble, so boiling them creates a chemical reaction, isomerization, that allows them to be soluble in water.

Aroma hops Hops that are used later in the boil for their bouquet, not their bitterness.

Astringent A drying, puckering taste. Can be negative or positive, depending on your taste buds.

Barley The predominant cereal grain used to make beer. Besides water, it's the biggest ingredient in brewing.

Barrel The standard term of measurement for brewing. A barrel equals 31 gallons. A half barrel, which is what you'll see stacked up at breweries, holds 15.5 gallons.

Berliner weisse This ghostly pale, low-alcohol German wheat beer typically gets its acidic tang from *Lactobacillus* bacteria. Drink it straight, or do as the Germans do and add a shot of sweet syrup (*mit Schuss*) and slurp it through a straw.

Bittering hops Used early in the boil to add bitterness, not aroma.

Boil This is the stage in beer making when the wort is boiled in order to kill bacteria and yeast, as well as to cause proteins to coagulate. Hops are added during this stage.

Bottle conditioned Beer that's naturally carbonated by live yeast lurking within the bottle.

Brewers Association Based in Boulder, Colorado, this trade organization is the country's preeminent craft beer advocate. It curates Denver's annual Great American Beer Festival.

Brew kettle The vessel in which the wort is boiled with hops.

Brut IPA An IPA variant made by using amylase enzyme. It converts starches into the simple sugar glucose that yeast readily consumes, leaving behind little residual sweetness. The result is a kindling-dry beer named after brut, the second-driest Champagne classification.

Cask ale Also called *real ale*, cask ale is unfiltered, naturally carbonated beer that's best served at fifty-five degrees Fahrenheit, which plays up its subtler flavors and aromas.

Cicerone A beer sommelier who passes the Cicerone Certification Program. The four levels are certified beer server, Certified Cicerone, Advanced Cicerone, and Master Cicerone; there are only eighteen Master Cicerones as of January 2019.

Coolship Imagine a shallow, oversized baking pan, big enough to make brownies for one thousand friends. That's a coolship. Brewers fill the vessel with steamy wort that, as it cools, attracts native yeast and bacteria. See **Spontaneous Fermentation**.

Craft beer It pretty much means nothing, as useless a descriptor as *artisanal* and *handcrafted*.

Craft brewer A nebulous, controversial, confusing term that, according to the Brewers Association, denotes a small, independent brewery that makes fewer than six million barrels of beer a year. Many microbreweries are no longer micro, so *independent brewery* is the preferred term for, well, brewers that remained independent. Things are complicated.

Crowler A 32-ounce canned growler that can be filled up with beer, à la a glass growler.

Decoction mashing A portion of wort is drawn off and boiled to create dark polymers called melanoidins, also found in coffee and bread crust. The boiled wort is blended back into the beer, contributing a richly complex malt character. Decoction mashing is often utilized to create Czech pilsners, most notably Pilsner Urquell.

DDH The acronym stands for double dry-hopped, which signifies an IPA with an extra amount of dry-hopping.

Double IPA A stronger, more intense IPA; typically, the ground floor sits around 8 percent ABV. See **Imperial IPA**.

Dry-hopping Hops that are added to beer that has finished fermenting or is conditioning. This step creates the intense aromatics that have defined modern beer.

Fermentation The metabolic process during which yeasts devour the sugars like ants at a picnic, creating alcohol and carbon dioxide.

Filtration The removal of all the floating proteins and yeast, creating a clearer, more stable—and sometimes less flavorful—beer.

Fresh hop beer A fragrant beer made with the year's first batches of dried hops.

Great American Beer Festival The Super Bowl of American brewing since 1982. More than two thousand brewers enter the Denver competition to medal in more than one hundred categories.

Gueuze This traditional Belgian beer is made by blending one-, two-, and three-year-old lambics, then letting the mixture age and continue fermenting in the bottle. The result is a dry, fruity elixir with a lip-scrunching sourness.

Hazy IPA A soft, fragrant, and totally opaque approach that swaps bitterness for intensified aromas and flavors that are often described as "juicy" and "fruity." The style is also called New England IPA, because of its birthplace in the Northeast.

Hop The creeping bine (a bine climbs by wrapping its stem around a support, as compared with a vine, which climbs with tendrils or suckers) *Humulus lupulus*, whose female flowers (called cones) flavor beers and provide bitterness. Each variety has its own unique flavor profile. Hop resins possess two primary acids, alpha and beta. Beta acids contribute to a beer's bouquet. Alpha acids serve as a preservative and contribute bitterness when hops are added early in the boil, flavor later in the boil, and aroma in the last minutes of a boil. Here's an important note: hops smell like marijuana because the plants are related, paving the path for an interconnected future.

Hop creep A phenomenon that occurs when excessive usage of hops rekindles fermentation, raising levels of carbonation and alcohol and potentially creating off flavors.

Imperial IPA A stronger, more intense IPA; often used interchangeably with *double IPA*, but the alcohol content may reach double digits, putting it closer to triple IPA territory.

India pale ale (IPA) A hop-intensified style of beer that has become craft brewing's missionary, converting drinkers worldwide. A double IPA, triple IPA, or even quadruple IPA increases the hops and malt, creating a stronger beer that may be either intensely bitter or soft and fragrant. See **Hazy IPA**.

International bitterness unit (IBU) A scientific scale that measures bitterness in beer. A low IBU (Budweiser is around 11) means the beer isn't hoppy; when an IBU tops triple digits, you're in for a mouth-scrunching ride. However, IBU is not a perfect measure of bitterness. A 5 percent IPA with 50 IBUs will be leagues more intense than a 10 percent IPA with 50 IBUs.

Kellerbier An unfiltered German ale or lager christened after the cold cellars (*keller* is German for "cellar") where the beers were traditionally matured. Kellerbier is closely linked to zwickelbier, an unfiltered German lager named after the *zwickel* ("zv-ick-el"), or valve, that brewers use to sample beer. The slight difference: kellerbiers are a bit more assertive.

Kettle sour A quickly produced sour beer made with lactic acid bacteria, most commonly *Lactobacillus*. You'll know kettle sours by their tart, lemony profile, and affordable price tag.

Kveik Norwegian farmhouse yeast that ferments like a champ at temperatures in excess of ninety degrees Fahrenheit.

Lager The second main style of beer. Like penguins, bottom-fermenting lager yeasts prefer cooler temperatures. They also take longer to ferment, hence the term *lager*; *lagern* means "to rest" in German. Lagers are typically crisp, delicate, and as refreshing as an August plunge in a Maine lake.

Lambic Made with wheat, this traditional Belgian beer is spontaneously fermented with wild yeasts, resulting in a sour, tart, barnyard-leaning profile. Lambics can broken down into three general classes: those made with fruit such as cherries (kriek), raspberries (framboise), or black currants (cassis); gueuze, which is a blend of young and old lambics; and faro, a lambic sweetened with candi or brown sugar.

Malt To create malt, cereal grains are bathed in water. This jump-starts germination, allowing the grain to create the enzymes required to convert starches and proteins into fermentable sugars. The process is arrested when maltsters—the people who make malt—heat and dry the grain. Like coffee, grain can be roasted to create different flavors and intensities.

Mash The initial step in brewing. Crushed grain is steeped in a big ol' pot of boiling water, transforming starches into sugars.

Mash tun The vessel in which brewers boil their mash.

Mobile canning Instead of buying a canning machine, breweries hire canning companies to travel to their facilities to package beer.

Mouthfeel How the beer feels when you drink it—a combination of body, texture, carbonation, and flavor. Mouthfeel is as subjective as a Yelp review.

Noble hops European hop varieties that are aromatic and less bitter. That's not necessarily negative. These hops, including Hallertauer, Tettnanger, Spalt, and Saaz, impart a spicy, herbal, zesty character. Commonly found in pilsners and European lagers.

Oats The grain supplies beer with a creaminess comparable to a whole-milk latté.

Oxidation When beer is exposed to oxygen, it undergoes a series of chemical reactions that create stale flavors sometimes described as "sherry" or "cardboard."

Pasteurization Murdering yeast through a serious application of heat. Unpasteurized beers retain their yeast, which means the beer will continue to evolve over time.

Pastry stout Slang used to describe the sugary wave of beers inspired by cakes, candies, cookies, and other desserts. Credit for the phrase's origin goes to comedian Alex Kidd, of the website Don't Drink Beer.

Pilsner In the 1840s, this lager variant style was born in the Czech Republic town of PlzeĐ, aka Pilsen. The straw-gold brew is see-through and packs plenty of spicy floral notes and zingy bitterness—the trademark of the noble hops used to brew pilsners.

Priming Dosing a fermented beer with priming sugar after it has been bottled or kegged, spurring increased carbonation and flavor creation.

Saison Originally brewed to slake the thirst of Belgian farmhands, earthy, spicy saisons inhabit a wide stylistic range—some are fruity, while others are desert-dry, peppery, and aromatic. Often called a farmhouse ale.

Session beer Beer low in alcohol, not in flavor. Best for sipping during a long-haul drinking session.

Skunked When UV light strikes beer, it causes isohumulones—chemicals released when hops are boiled—to break down, creating chemical compounds identical to those found in skunk spray. Never buy a beer sunbathing in a store's window.

Sour It's a description, not a style of beer.

Spontaneous fermentation A process by which brewers cool wort in large, shallow pans and then allow ambient yeast and bacteria to settle into the sugary water. The inoculated beer is then transferred to wooden barrels, where time and microbes then make their magic happen.

Table beer Food-friendly beer that accompanies meals and conversation and is rarely the focal point. Originally from Belgium.

Triple IPA A herculean IPA heaped with hops. No hard-and-fast definition applies, but a solid rule of thumb is that triple IPAs are stronger than 10 percent ABV.

Wheat Used in brewing, the grain contributes a smooth character, hazy hue, and touch of tartness.

Wild beer A catchall category of beers dosed with the wild yeast *Brettanomyces*, which creates complex flavors that could be rustic and earthy, or even tropical. Brewers often coferment with a souring bacteria like *Lactobacillus* and *Pediococcus*, a process called mixed fermentation.

World Beer Cup A high-status, biannual beer competition open to breweries worldwide.

Wort The hot soup that's extracted from the mash. It's an all-you-can-eat buffet for the yeasts that create beer.

Yeast The microscopic critters that craft your favorite beverage and make any hour just a little bit happier. Grains and hops notwithstanding, yeast drives the lion's share of a beer's flavor profile. Each strain provides a different flavor profile, and breweries often cultivate their own idiosyncratic yeast strains.

INDEX

ABOUT THE AUTHOR

Joshua M. Bernstein is a beer, spirits, food, and travel journalist and the fast-typing author of *Brewed Awakening*, *The Complete Beer Course*, *Complete IPA*, and *Homebrew World* (all Sterling Epicure). But that's not all! His work appears regularly in newspapers, magazines, and websites, including *The New York Times*, *Men's Journal*, *New York*, *Wine Enthusiast*, and *Imbibe*, where, as contributing editor, he oversees beer coverage. He talks about beer on the radio, podcasts, and TV a bunch, staying sane by biking around New York City in search of delicious dumplings and beer, as well as boogie-boarding at Rockaway Beach. He lives with his wife in Brooklyn, surrounded by many plants and their daughter, Violet. He's pretty good at keeping things alive. Find him on Twitter and Instagram @JoshMBernstein.

IMAGE CREDITS

BEER FLAVOR MAP

SECOND EDITION

FRUITY

CITRUS
GRAPEFRUIT
ORANGE
LEMON
LIME

TROPICAL
MANGO
PINEAPPLE
PAPAYA
BANANA
LYCHEE
GUAVA
PASSION FRUIT
COCONUT

BERRY
RASPBERRY
STRAWBERRY
BLUEBERRY
BLACKBERRY
CONCORD GRAPE
MUSCAT GRAPE
GOOSEBERRY
BLACK CURRANT/CATTY
RED CURRANT

MELON
CANTALOUPE
HONEYDEW
CUCUMBER
WATERMELON

STONE FRUIT
PEACH
APRICOT
NECTARINE
CHERRY
PLUM

POMME
GREEN APPLE
RED APPLE
PEAR
CIDER

DRIED FRUIT
PRUNE
FIG
DATE
RAISIN

FLORAL
GERANIUM
ROSE
CITRONELLA
LAVENDER
LILAC
CHAMOMILE
HONEYSUCKLE
JASMINE
LILY
VIOLET
PERFUME

STALE
LEATHER
PAPER
CARDBOARD
WAXY
GOAT HAIR
WET DOG
MEATY/SOY SAUCECE

SWEET AROMATIC
CARAMEL
HONEY
TOFFEE
CHOCOLATE
BROWN SUGAR
BURNT SUGAR
MOLASSES
VANILLA
BUBBLEGUM
FROSTING
MARSHMALLOW
PIE CRUST
MAPLE SYRUP
COLA

SPICY
BLACK PEPPER
WHITE PEPPER
NUTMEG
ALLSPICE
CLOVE
JUNIPER
LICORICE/ANISE
CORIANDER
CINNAMON
GINGER
CARAWAY

DAIRY
BUTTER
BUTTERSCOTCH
SOUR MILK
CHEESE
YOGURT

HERB-ACEOUS
BLACK TEA
GREEN TEA
MINT
ROSEMARY
DILL
THYME

ROTTEN
SWEAT
BOILED EGG
ROTTEN GARBAGE
FECAL
BABY VOMIT
ROTTEN CHEESE
FISH
LIGHTSTRUCK/SKUNKY
ROTTEN VEGETABLE

TASTE
SWEET
SALTY
SOUR
BITTER
UMAMI
FAT

AROM
FLAV